PAT WELLINGTON

Published Aug 28, 2017

D0162325

Effective People Management

Your guide to boosting performance, managing conflict and becoming a great leader in your start up

2ND EDITION

KoganPage

First published in Great Britain and the United States in 2011 by Kogan Page Limited
Second edition 2017

2nd Floor, 45 Gee Street	c/o Martin P Hill Consulting	4737/23 Ansari Road
London	122 W 27th St, 10th Floor	Daryaganj
EC1V 3RS	New York, NY 10001	New Delhi 110002
United Kingdom	USA	India

© Pat Wellington 2017

The right of Pet Wellington to be identified as the author of this work has been asserted by her in accordance with the Copyright, Designs and Patents Act 1988.

ISBN   978 0 7494 8082 0
E-ISBN   978 0 7494 8083 7

British Library Cataloguing-in-Publication Data

A CIP record for this book is available from the British Library.

Typeset by Integra Software Services, Pondicherry
Print production managed by Jellyfish
Printed and bound by CPI Group (UK) Ltd, Croydon CR0 4YY

CONTENTS

To Rosemary and Ginger

PREFACE

Twenty years from now you will be disappointed by the things you did not do, so throw off the bowlines, sail away from a safe harbour, catch the trade winds in your sails. Explore. Dream. Discover. MARK TWAIN

Being an entrepreneur can be captivating and energizing as you develop your ideas for a new product or service. But then you come to the people stage of getting your business off the ground and this is not always easy. Perhaps you have written a business plan, secured funds and are ready for a new product launch; you will ultimately need to move on to employ others to help build your company. Equally well, you might already have grown to become an SME but find the people management side of things challenging. Well, this book is for you. Its aim is to show you how to lead and manage others, understand what part of the workload to pass over and how to do this, and in turn build on your own strengths and the entrepreneurial spirit that got you to where you are today.

Management of others can be downright difficult. It doesn't just happen. Hoping others perform doesn't work. Why? Because we are all under pressure. Stress is commonplace in the organizational vocabulary. There never seems to be sufficient resources or time. To top it all, an entrepreneur's objectives often appear to be in conflict. For example, how do you deliver the desired results *and*:

- recruit the right calibre of person / people to build your company when you want to keep hold of certain activities
- be decisive and yet encourage participation
- inspire and motivate yet listen
- decide and delegate
- get your work done and maintain a work–life balance

- communicate bad news and show you care?

I have written this book for anyone who wants answers to the above.

A simple definition of management is: the achievement of results through other people. Because you cannot do everything yourself, it follows that you will stand or fall by the success of those you employ or your ability to work with others. As management guru Peter Drucker said, 'The basic task of management is to make people productive.' This book explains how. It will help anyone who wants to get the right balance between delivering desired results through other people and working with others and still successfully manage productivity, efficiency, effectiveness and financial measures, etc. You may need to work with a variety of different resources to make this possible – but one factor is common: people. I deliver training and coaching sessions internationally working with a broad cross-section of managers be they entrepreneurs or working within an SME or blue chip organization. Wherever I go I'm always asked a variation of the same questions:

- I am a start-up. How is it best to build my business? Should I recruit specialists to run their own team? Or would it be best if I recruit a task-oriented team that I manage myself?

- When building my business and recruiting new staff I want to ensure that I pick winners. How robust does the recruitment process need to be to give me the best chance of doing this?

- What makes an effective leader?

- What is the difference between leadership and management?

- Where do great managers get their power from? How can I tap into this and use it productively?

- How do I create a vision that people can relate to and find inspirational?

- I know as an entrepreneur I need to take on a strategic role, how do I do this and pass on day-to-day operational issues without things falling apart?

- OK, OK! I know it is important to train and develop employees, but budgets are really stretched right now. Apart from sending people on a training course, which takes people out of the workplace for several days, what other cost-effective options are there for their development?

- Performance management is obviously a key part of my role. What is the best way to monitor performance, and set standards for people to achieve?

- I am sure once I put a team together that they will go through a rocky period. As the leader of the team, how can I get people back on track and working more harmoniously together?

- During problem solving and quality improvement activities there is a need to get people to think more expansively, find new approaches, and be more creative. How can I get them to do this?

- I work for an SME and due to Brexit unfortunately need to make redundancies. What should I do?

- Dealing with people problems is a challenge. Give me a range of approaches that I can use, according to the situation that I need to handle.

These questions, with their answers, have been used as the foundation stone for this book.

It starts by looking at big-picture considerations: leadership qualities that inspire people, and how to manage and motivate them. Once your business has started to grow you will need to look at recruiting others. This can be a challenging time as those that you recruit and how you structure your company can make all the difference between success and failure. This book will give you options as to how to create the appropriate structure that will work for you. Tied in to this will be your recruitment strategy. And as this is key for entrepreneurs a robust chapter has been created to give you step by step guidelines through the whole process.

Your role as a manager of others is also covered, and the importance of creating a learning environment. The second part of the book explores day-to-day management. This starts by looking at typical activities in your working day – undertaking tasks and projects, delegation, and attending and running meetings. It then moves on to performance management and the recognition and reward process. Problems arise in any company or team, be these interpersonal or operational, and a chapter is dedicated to each of these issues. We are trading in difficult economic times, and tough decisions might need to be made, including making people redundant. This topic is covered from various angles. Above all else the book has a realistic and positive attitude to help entrepreneurs stand on their own two feet as soon as possible. It's certainly not full of gobbledegook, just plain English.

In planning and writing this book I have tried to keep in mind a vision of the potential reader. I see you as a busy entrepreneur looking to build your business or a manager trying to get the best from your team, and requiring fast access to pragmatic information and proven experience. Possibly you will dip in and out of the book as you need to. You might access it from the index rather than from the list of contents. I imagine you will not have a great deal of time to spare and so I have given key information about a topic, followed by what I am calling 'tips and techniques' – a range of options and ideas for you to select and try, plus case studies to see things in action, and assessment instruments to use.

So here we go. I hope you find this book an informative, practical guide that is useful in your everyday working activities.

ACKNOWLEDGEMENTS

This book is the product of many people's minds and efforts. Each has contributed insight, facts, experience, introductions and personal support during its preparation. My contacts in companies around the world who have embraced change have willingly given time and access to information. This has helped me understand and record in these pages best-practice approaches together with a step-by-step overview of how to handle all the day-to-day activities that entrepreneurs and managers in SMEs and start-ups need to undertake to deliver outstanding performance.

I wish to thank my friends and consultant colleagues who have shared with me their experience and knowledge and contributed case studies used in this book. A specific thank you to Owen Green, business consultant, Barbara Hawker, Managing Director, Hurst Associates Europe, Edward Kirwan, founder of Eddie's Doggy Daycare, Rebecca Gregory, CEO of Thinking Bob, and Mary Reggie De Silva, my management consultant colleague from Kuala Lumpur, for sharing with me their experiences.

A special thank you to two of my consultant colleagues, Patrick Forsyth and Niall Foster, who have been there over several years encouraging and supporting me during my consultancy and training assignments.

Last, and by no means least, my publisher Anna Moss and her colleagues from Kogan Page who have guided me on practical matters during the creation of this material.

ABOUT THE AUTHOR

Pat Wellington is a popular international speaker and busy consultant. Her specialism is leadership, the management of change and team building, communication skills and customer care.

She has published *Kaizen Strategies for Customer Care* and was a contributor to *Kaizen Strategies for Improving Team Performance*. In 2009 her book *Effective Team Leadership Handbook for Engineers* was be published, and in 2010 *Effective Customer Care* was released as part of the *Sunday Times* Creating Success series. In 2011 *The Sunday Times* and Kogan Page published the first edition of this book, *Effective People Management*, and in 2012 *Managing Successful Teams*. She has written many articles for management publications, and been a guest speaker at conferences and seminars in the UK, Gulf and South East Asia.

Pat started her working life as a general manager in the retail sector. Twenty years ago she moved into consultancy, initially joining City University, and then moved on to head up the Management Development Unit of London Metropolitan University, the largest educational establishment in London. In recent years she has worked as an independent consultant specializing in the best of East and West management practices. The consultancy and training assignments she has undertaken have been numerous and diverse in most industry sectors, including health care, manufacturing, IT, and the service sector, plus a variety of government bodies. She is an enthusiastic and motivational facilitator and has helped leaders and managers to gain skills and knowledge, and importantly become more productive on returning to their workplace.

In the UK she has worked for blue chips such as Canon and Coates Viyella, private hospital chains – the Nuffield and the St Martin's hospital groups – and in the government sector she has project-managed MBA programmes. In Europe she has worked with three United Nations agencies in Rome and the UNHCR in Geneva.

Also within Europe she has undertaken a major research assignment for Coca-Cola. In the Gulf Pat has delivered sessions and keynote presentations for petrochemical organizations, the Government of Dubai and Zamil Steel. In South-East Asia she regularly delivers seminars for the Institute of Management in Singapore, and delivers programmes in KL and Indonesia.

If you would like to share any of your leadership or management experiences with Pat she would welcome hearing from you. Contact her at **pat@pwellington.plus.com**

Leadership

Introduction

It all begins with a dream to fly higher and stand out with a difference. Every entrepreneur believes they can offer something different to the marketplace. Why otherwise should they start to trade? The stark reality sets in within the first year of going it alone. The statistics aren't exactly encouraging. Recent research by Ormsby Street, a company set up in the UK in November 2014 to help small businesses blighted by late payment and cash flow issues, states that 91 per cent of UK start-ups survive their first year but only 40 per cent will last to their fifth year of trading (Donnelly, 2016). Companies in the information and communications industry have the best chance of surviving the first year. Those in the health sector are most likely to still be in existence five years on. So what is to be done to ensure your company is one of those positive statistics?

In volatile times, which we are surely in, the firm response to uncertain economic conditions and markets should be to take stock – and then take action. The worst possible reaction is one of shell shock: wishing that conditions will change, that difficulties will go away and believing that there is nothing to do but wait. Most often waiting for things to get back to normal is simply not an option. Things change – and they certainly change, sometimes radically and quickly, when uncertainty affects economic prospects. And people must change too.

One thing is constant: the only antidote to any problem in an organization is people – who they are, how they operate, what ideas they have and how effectively they work. Managing people is a challenge, but it is essential. How well it is done makes a difference and a well-managed team will always outperform others less well directed.

Hence this book. The focus is on entrepreneurs, those starting and managing businesses. But perhaps every manager needs an entrepreneurial streak and, however innovative an organization may be, how those managing its people operate is a key differentiating factor in its success.

Mark Zuckerberg, Richard Branson and Richard Dyson are household names to entrepreneurs and consumers alike, and they all had to start somewhere. They knew how to create a product that was unique to the marketplace, that they believed in and that consumers wanted to use or buy. That was the foundation for building their company. But they could not do this on their own. They had to employ and work with others to build their business. This is where leadership and management come into the equation.

As an entrepreneur what is your role as a leader?

In the most basic terms the response to the question 'What is leadership?' it is a relatively simple one in my book – it's an innate ability to motivate, influence and lead people towards a common goal or purpose.

There are certain fundamental competencies that you should have or develop. Number one is tenacity, to never give up – being an entrepreneur is not for the weak-hearted. You need to be aware of the big picture – the global stage is changing, with for example Brexit and President Trump. Regulatory requirements and trading conditions will be revised and changed. You also need to have commercial drive to be able to win in the marketplace using your superior knowledge, strategic partnerships and your entrepreneurial flair. What we have seen in the marketplace with many entrepreneurs is their ability to create and build something from practically nothing. They have a knack for sensing an opportunity where others see chaos, contradiction and confusion, and we salute them for this capacity. And of course you also need management competencies in planning, budgeting, recruiting, organizing and problem solving to start off with in order to create and maintain efficient processes and day-to-day business operations. In time as your company develops and expands you can delegate many of these responsibilities but if you are in a start-up this is down to you.

In the different stages of development of your company you will call on your different skills and competencies.

At the start-up stage creativity will almost certainly be your driving force. Creativity can take many forms from developing the product or service through to the use of limited resources, and having the ability to catch a potential investor's eye.

Stage two as you start to grow means your need to be able to articulate your direction in measurable goals. This is not just financial goals, but also having a clear idea about your target market, and articulating your vision in a sentence that is measurable, inspiring and achievable. And as your business develops you will need to re-define your direction as circumstances change – this could be changes in the marketplace and its demands, resource changes or new investors coming on board.

You will reach a certain point when you simply won't be able to do everything yourself and will need to hire others to build your business. Delegation skills will be key.

As the business grows further you will need to get cohesion and collaboration between those who immediately report into you to ensure that a silo mentality does not start to happen with these key members of staff. Your role at this stage should be far more externally focused. In promoting your brand or service one of your options is to become a 'thought leader'. Establish yourself as an authority by speaking, writing and hosting webinars. You should also seek out more traditional platforms such as becoming a guest speaker at industry specific events.

And finally strategic thinking comes in to its own at each stage of development. Your role will be to build alliances with suppliers, customers, and new business partners.

Practicalities to move forward

So let's get down to details. As a leader you need to do these things:

1 Develop a vision that creates an appropriate and compelling way forward for the future. Where are we going? What is our goal? As you grow the business the most important/difficult thing for leaders is to bring this vision or 'sense' into the management team they select. Their role is to communicate this concrete framework to the team, to create shared meaning and understanding.

2 Set strategy and turn it into actionable plans. What framework (not tools) do we use to get there?

3 Organize the structure of your company and establish and maintain relationships with all key stakeholders to enable success. Shape and strengthen the organization to create long-term sustainability. Decide who can best help you get there.

4 Who is best for the job and can help others be successful? Excellent leaders can't do it alone. It's the people they choose.

5 Prepare the culture – what attitude and behaviour should we have?

A fundamental part of the leader's role is to inspire their people to deliver the business vision. This, and the following, are all soundly based on what the organization needs to succeed. This may include:

- establishing and communicating a vision to provide a context;
- motivation and clarity for those who support the leader;
- engendering a passion for organizational values in others;
- acting as an ambassador for the brand;
- meeting the challenges of driving the business.

The importance of organizational values

Commitment to, and pursuit of, the vision and values helps leaders to shape their ideas and guides their actions. All too often values are listed on an organization's website and forgotten. This shouldn't be the case. Organizational values guide leaders' daily actions. Values are guiding beliefs about how things should be done. Values are about passion. Their goal is to give stakeholders 100 per cent and inspire staff to do the same. Values help people to prioritize and make the right decisions when they are faced with tough situations. They give a shared belief and way of behaving that brings all employees together and sets the organization apart from its competitors. I'd suggest some examples of values might be:

- **Passion for customers.** Our customers choose us and trust us. In return we must strive to anticipate and understand their needs and delight them with our service.

- **Passion for our people.** Outstanding people working together make our organization exceptionally successful.

- **Passion for results.** We are action-oriented and driven by a desire to be the best.

- **Passion for our environment/community.** We will help our customers to have fuller lives – both through the services we provide and through the impact we have on the environment around us.

CASE STUDY   Zappos' 10 core values

Zappos Shoes CEO is Tony Hsieh, who made the transition from being an investor in the company to this role in 2000. Since that time he has transformed the company from $1.6 million to $1 billion. So how has he done this in the most unlikely of environments – selling shoes on the internet? He believes passionately that customer service and creating an environment based on ten core values has been the key to the company's success.

These core values are:

1 Deliver WOW through service.

2 Embrace and drive change.

3 Create fun and a little weirdness.

4 Be adventurous, creative and open-minded.

5 Pursue growth and learning.

6 Build honest and open relationships with communication.

7 Build a positive team and family spirit.

8 Do more with less.

9 Be passionate and determined.

10 Be humble.

These are not the most classic core values for a company, but in his view having a core value such as 'being humble' is important. He does not want to be surrounded on a daily basis by people who are too egotistical. So how has he managed to create a company that offers great customer service – something that every organization claims to do, but rarely achieves?

Firstly, he puts importance on the nature of people that are hired to work in their call centre. They don't have to be passionate about shoes, but they do have to be passionate about customer service. He believes that skills can be trained, but you can't do that with attitude. New recruits receive at least four weeks of training, exploring cultural issues as well as tools and customer service techniques. Staff who are recruited for other posts in the organization not only have to be technically proficient for the job, but also are considered to be suitable for culturally fitting in with the company's ethos.

As far as service to the customer is concerned, they offer free shipping each way, with a return policy of up to 365 days. The call centre is also open 24 hours a day, manned by staff who are encouraged to relate to customers in a normal, friendly way, rather than reading from a script. They also put on all their documentation a free helpline, prominently displayed, as they want to get feedback from their customers.

Times have not always been rosy. In 2007–08 there was an economic downturn, and the financial planning of the company was based on growth, so they needed to lay off staff. This was done in an open and transparent way, with those being made redundant offered two months' severance, and employees who had been there for longer than three years being offered a month's pay for every year they had worked at the company, plus continued health plan provision.

You can find out more about this dynamic company, and see other examples of best practice by going to the excellent website MeetTheBoss TV at **www.meettheboss.tv**.

Closely aligned to core values is the need for companies to 'do the right thing' – to be ethical and show social responsibility.

Doing the right thing in business

Increasingly in the business world ethical behaviour and trading ethically is becoming not only important to the customer but also to your trading partners. Mike Clasper, President of Business Development at Proctor & Gamble, once said: 'People are going to want to find out about the citizenship of a brand, whether it is doing the right thing socially, economically and environmentally.' While the need for ethical behaviour is clear, its definition may not be so. Many organizations ask their employees to sign employee proprietary guidelines, which define the values and ethical and social responsibilities employees have to customers, competitors and suppliers as well as their organization. Ethics and social responsibility tries to address the complex and changing relationships employees may have to deal with. As always, no rulebook covers all possible situations. None of us can foresee changes, in industry or in society, which may lie around the corner. For you as an entrepreneur you need to instil in those that you employ that they apply their ethical and social responsibilities to the best of their ability in their own individual situation.

Organizations depend on employees to do the right thing; right for the employee and the company. After all, the organization's reputation is in each employee's hands. The importance of this subject is growing. For example, since 2010 courses in corporate social responsibility (CSR), ethics, sustainability or business and society are now required teaching in 66 per cent of business schools, up from 34 per cent in 2001. Employees quickly learn their organization's operating values or they may not survive for long. To the extent that they differ from stated values, the organization will suffer not only from doing things less effectively, but also from the cynicism of its members, who may use this as a reason for mistrusting the leadership.

Defining values, ethics and social responsibility

Earlier we spoke about personal values. In terms of ethics and social responsibility, values are what your profession judges to be right.

Individually or organizationally, values determine what is right and what is wrong, and doing what is right or wrong is what is meant by ethics. To behave ethically is to behave in a manner generally consistent with what is right or moral. However, what does 'generally considered to be right' actually mean? That is a critical question, and part of the difficulty in deciding whether or not behaviour is ethical is in determining what is right or wrong. Organizations, to a greater extent, define what is right or wrong for the members of the organization. Ethical codes, such as the US army's 'A cadet will not lie, cheat, or steal, or tolerate those who do', make clear what the organization considers to be right or wrong. For example, typical code of conduct principles should be unequivocal statements of what the organization considers to be ethical behaviour. An example might be:

> ### Example   Code of conduct
>
> 1 We act in the best interests of the organization and value our reputation.
> 2 We act with honesty and integrity.
> 3 We treat others with respect, value difference and maintain a safe working environment.
> 4 We identify conflicts of interest and manage them responsibly.
> 5 We respect and maintain privacy and confidentiality.
> 6 We do not make or receive improper payments, benefits or gains.
> 7 We comply with this Code, the law in territories in which we operate and our policies and procedures.
> 8 We immediately report any breaches of the Code, the law or our eight policies and procedures.

What does 'considers to be right' mean? All one needs to do is to look at the positive values of society and the organizations one belongs to, and what is right or wrong should be evident. There is another aspect to be considered, however, and that is the influence of societal or organizational norms. Norms are the unstated rules, usually informally reached by the members of a group, which govern the behaviour of the group's members. Norms often have a greater effect on what is and isn't done by the members of a group than formal rules and regulations.

The reason norms are important for a discussion of ethics and social responsibility is that norms may allow or even encourage certain behaviour as 'OK' that is not in keeping with society's or an organization's stated values. When there is a disconnect between stated and operating values, it may be difficult to determine what is 'right'.

An example might be a company that has among its stated values to treat everyone with dignity and respect, but whose norms have permitted and perhaps even encouraged a pattern of bullying over a number of years. Do those in the organization know that the behaviour is wrong, but condone it nevertheless? The recent banking crisis has led to a debate over state bailouts for banks that still pay staff huge bonuses. That's why many organizations now assess performance not only in terms of what is achieved, but how they achieve it – consistent with their values, code of ethics and risk/compliance/behaviour policies and standards.

Examples **Breaches of values, ethics and social responsibility**

- Fails to record a recordable gift or entertainment in an appropriate register.
- Fails to disclose a conflict of interest.
- Not reporting internal fraud to internal investigations.
- Fails to meet health and safety responsibilities.
- Not addressing issues raised by an audit in a timely, responsive and focused manner, possibly resulting in overdue audits.
- Receives adverse audit results for issues within their area of accountability.
- Takes inappropriate or unauthorized risks, for example by exceeding the relevant approved discretion.
- Fails to maintain sufficient levels of control and take personal accountability for all areas and associated processes within their area of responsibility.
- Fails to comply with relevant business processes (eg maintaining appropriate files, processes for maintaining customer information).
- Bullies, harasses or victimizes someone in the workplace.

- Treats someone less favourably or discriminates on the basis of an attribute such as sex, age, sexual orientation, disability, race, religion, ethnic origin etc.

- Views, accesses, stores and/or distributes inappropriate or offensive material via email or on the internet.

- Receives a customer complaint for poor treatment such as using inappropriate language, or being rude or dismissive.

So what's to be done?

Leaders need to provide a sense of direction and purpose. Individual team member values and the organization's values, ethics and sense of social responsibility should be in harmony if individuals want to move towards the vision. When someone says 'That's the way I am' as a reason for action or inaction, leaders must ask themselves if their staff believe their organization's vision and values only concern is to maximize organizational profits, and if this is the case how does it limit the possibilities of aligning personal with organization goals?

There is growing recognition of the limitations of assuming that people are just economic 'resources' interested in delivering profits. This has major implications for theory in economics and also the impact on people where technology, global competition, downsizing and re-engineering have created a workforce of employees seeking value, support and meaning in their lives.

Key tasks

- Does your mission statement clearly define the purpose of your company?
- Is your vision inspirational, measurable, and achievable?
- What core values do you want to instil in your company?

02

Growing your business from start-up

Introduction

Entrepreneurs can come from a variety of backgrounds. I don't want to risk putting people into strict categories but from my work over the years with start-ups and SMEs they have usually shown certain characteristics which reflect the background of the entrepreneur.

If the company has been set up by an accountant they are obviously competent at managing cash flow, outgoings and the admin side of the business, but could have less flair when it comes to generating new business and creating product ranges. On the other side of the coin, those that come from a sales and marketing background can win orders and generate revenue but could be less interested in controlling expenses and getting all the necessary systems and procedures in place for the company to sustain growth. So self-evidently in both these instances a counter balance person needs to be recruited. A great colleague of mine, Anita Roddick, the founder of The Body Shop, was an excellent front-of-house sales person, who could read the market well to bring new products into her shops each season. She also had a strong commitment to ecological and ethical issues, insisting that no products were tested on animals. Her mantra was 'Being good is good for business.' When they first set up their company her husband Gordon took care of the financial side of the business until they grew sufficiently to delegate responsibilities.

So in growing your business it's important to take a long hard look at your person strengths and weaknesses, and recruit to compensate the weaker areas. Several of the organizations we have worked with over the years have used various analysis methodologies during the growth stage of their business to be able to be more focused in whom they select to join them in the business. These analysis tools have included Thompson International Psychometric and Attitude Testing and the Myers Briggs Type Indicator.

Myers Briggs Type Indicator

The Myers Briggs Type Indicator (MBTI) uses the basis of Carl Jung's research into personality type preference and attempts to place it in the context of everyday lives, including work environments.

This type of personality exploration suggests that all individuals have two main attitudes (or orientations) and two predominant mental functions. Attitudes denote how an individual is likely to gain and direct their vitality or drive (extroversion or introversion) and how an individual is likely to be most comfortable living and organizing their existence (perceiving or judging). Mental functions on the other hand denote how a person prefers to assimilate new information (sensory or intuitive) and how this information is stored and accessed for the purposes of choice or decision (thinking or feeling).

Central to the theory is that all individuals have some degree of each of these four characteristics and that none of them is either right or wrong, it is simply the person we are by, often subconscious, preference. They are each something of a sliding scale for the vast majority of the population and individuals can, to some degree, choose to use an alternative style to their preference when occasion dictates. The MBTI preference indicator uses these types to give one of the 16 possible personality make-ups available, and offers a glimpse into some of our inner workings.

No one of the 16 personalities available is ever prevalent over another, as it is the interaction between and the understanding of them that helps us to develop business style and working practice. Those with an extraverted tendency may absorb and focus their energy from and toward others, or their outside environment, while those with an introverted tendency often prefer to source and direct their energy through reflection upon their inner self. Sensory information gatherers will tend to be detail oriented and give clear consideration to the current state of affairs, while intuitive information gatherers will attempt to elicit significance from patterns and look for further meaning in information presented. Those decisions makers with a preference for the thinking tendency may deploy reason and logic more often than those with a feeling tendency, who may opt to consider impact upon others and use more values based processes.

While it should be recognized that all of the characteristics identified in Myers Briggs research play a significant part in the development of a management style it is our experience that one of the most influential and often challenging is that of judging or perceiving. Interestingly, one of the predominant characteristics found in entrepreneurs is that of perceiving. A perceiving attitude is the type of character unlikely to conform to a classic management structure found in established businesses. They generally thrive in environments where open-ended decisions are constantly required and recognizing the necessity for change is part of everyday life. This characteristic is often the part of their identity that pushes an entrepreneur to work for themselves and be successful in developing unique business ideas.

Having strength in this characteristic has many business advantages, but the lack of the judging characteristic can result in an inability to relate to the need for structure as mentioned above. In a blue chip organization for example, an individual might lack this characteristic when they first move into employment, however, they will have the opportunity to develop this as they work their way through a more structured management environment.

The challenge for the entrepreneur as they grow their business is to develop a more holistic management style to meet the gap between a hierarchical and flat structure. Entrepreneurs in our experience are more often than not good at seeing the bigger picture, are visionaries – that is how they have become entrepreneurs in the first place. Their challenge then is to be able to see the individual capacity of those they employ to encourage and empower them in order to bring balances and checks to the whole business as it grows and develops.

Getting the structure of your company right

So in a start-up an entrepreneur could for example be one person and their dog working from a bedroom in their house. But as the business grows they can find themselves more and more involved in operational issues rather than working on what interests them, often R & D, product development and strategic planning.

Owen Green, a business consultant colleague of mine, believes they have numerous choices at this point, which can be widely grouped into two main categories.

The traditional option: They can introduce and develop a classic management structure, placing key appointments in operational, and financial management, therefore maintaining strategy for themselves. This has the advantage of giving two key lines of communication for the entrepreneur in to his or her business.

Often though, such forward thinking individuals may struggle with this route. Firstly when a business has been your 'baby', being able to find two single individuals with whom they can place this level of trust in understanding the overall aims and objectives of the business can seem impossible. Secondly, such key appointments may not offer complete job roles in a truly dynamic business, resulting in other elements being added ad hoc and reducing the overall performance of such specialist appointments. This can often result in the entrepreneur becoming frustrated as they backfill skill gaps themselves, taking them away from the part of the business they not only enjoy but also excel in.

The non-traditional or holistic option: They can continue to treat the business as the individual entity it already is, individualizing their recruitment strategy and overall structure to suit the needs of the enterprise.

This approach involves the entrepreneur considering their own strengths and the part of the business they enjoy managing, and in turn treating their weaknesses and the part of the business they do not enjoy as a skills deficit. At this point an entrepreneur could chose to work alongside a colleague they bring in to the business and who embodies the structure and constraints this brings in order to leave themselves free to a lead fulfilled working life. Inevitably we find that the majority of the colleagues introduced at this point in time tend to be high in the judging characteristic, but the fact that consideration has been given firstly to the business need and secondly to the specific skills this appointment requires means that the entrepreneur is far more likely to effectively appoint an opposite with whom they are comfortable working and ultimately trust.

This balance then allows both parties to manage a much more individualized structure. From what we have witnessed this style fosters an environment in which managers at all levels tend to be specialists within their area of expertise. These managers are in turn empowered to create their own teams in a style that best suits the needs of their particular business area and recognizes their own skills deficits as a tool for business growth rather than something they attempt to hide from their superiors. For example, as the business continues to grow those managers who demonstrate the judging characteristic have two options: they can either aim to increase their perceiving characteristic or employ those with this characteristic. This type of structure works exceptionally well providing that the managers are given both autonomy and expectations within the contribution to the overall business. Some businesses go so far as to directly link remuneration to these expectations, in the form of key performance indicators (KPIs).

The benefit to the overall business is that it is constantly moving forward much in the way of a cooperative, and is able to form and change at a great pace. This level of awareness of preferred ways of working, when fostered from the very start and regarded as valuable from the very top, seeps seamlessly into the culture of the business and can create the type of open-faced organization where employees and potential employees want to work.

To find out more about Myers Briggs check out their website www.myersbriggs.org.

So let's move on to look at a couple of start-up organizations and see how they have managed to grow their business.

CASE STUDY   Thinking Bob Ltd

Thinking Bob is an events-centred social networking organization, with a strong social media and technology focus and was set up in 2012. Based in London, they aim to tackle the everyday isolation created by living in a society where traditional community continues to slowly erode and there is an ever-increasing reliance upon technology to fill the void created. Deeply embedded within the company values are an understanding of the organization's social responsibility and a desire to help their client base of members to connect with other, likeminded, individuals on both personal and pseudo-personal platforms. The company has sustained continual growth throughout its lifespan but were recently challenged with the task of increasing subscription membership and market share within a price conscious, highly competitive marketplace.

With this in mind the senior management team undertook a detailed internal SWOT analysis to identify the areas that would aid and challenge the company's further development. From this work came a number of very clear indicators. Firstly, the Thinking Bob brand has a huge level of client loyalty. Its members are zealots about the product and whole heartedly support the community, often recognizing the value that the company has added to their personal lives. Secondly, the management team are very driven but share very similar characteristics in their working styles. This has been successful in aiding the community to grow, as all of the team share a real skill in personal interaction but could be limiting the formation of the type of structure required in a business of this size. Thirdly, the time investment being made by the management team in the delivery of events could be prohibiting the management of overall strategy, this in turn affecting the businesses ability to seek external financial investment and subsequent growth.

Accepting these outcomes the team developed a truly unique strategy. They recognized the value of the strong brand loyalty and their strong people skills and chose to open up lines of communication with the company's membership base. They asked prevalent questions regarding how members would like to see the organization grow and invited input in all aspects of the business from the members. The result of this was quite remarkable. The company benefited from an influx of offers from members to assist them on a voluntary basis. As a result they were able to improve the technology that supports the business, extend their presence within social media platforms, increase their events team to treble the number of events being offered on a monthly basis, create new events with increased certainty of success and improve overall business administration. The team managed the development of a range of new working models, to connect this support with the business need.

At this point structure for the business began to fall into place quite holistically and increased levels of external investment and subsequent growth quickly followed. Moreover, the skill base available to the business increased and the community actually strengthened, due to increased client involvement.

From this case study it is evident that the strength of entrepreneur lead SME is often found within their ability to think differently. Entrepreneurs, while often feeling challenged by perceived norms and restrictive structure, are more readily able to adapt and change in a fast and dynamic manner. Introducing new ideas is often second nature to this type of business leader and harnessing this tendency, while balancing it with strong interpersonal skills and a willingness to listen, can yield unprecedented results. Harmonizing a businesses need to conform and become structured with its ability to remain individual can be a key driver to its success.

CASE STUDY   Eddie's Doggy Daycare Ltd

Eddie's Doggy Daycare, founded in 2014, was the brainchild of its founder, Edward Kirwan, whose understanding of the importance of pet ownership and its benefits to the well-being of individuals led him to begin to consider the well-being of pets, specifically dogs. Dogs often suffer from a lack of socialization and sufficient levels of exercise due to constraints of owners, who are attempting to balance a busy modern life. As a true entrepreneur Edward's belief in his product led him to give up his existing job, with a large blue chip organization, to follow this new direction.

This life-changing experience is certainly not for the faint-hearted. He started with just a handful of clients and worked tirelessly, quickly developing a fruitful and profitable business. This stage of business development is often regarded as the most difficult. Few of us can imagine taking the leap of faith involved and many fail to complete the journey, but what happens after this stage is particularly interesting.

How does an entrepreneur move from a single-handed approach to the inclusion of other colleagues, employing staff and seeking advice on the areas of the business that are potentially beyond their skill set? Quite simply, there is no categorical answer to this question. An entrepreneur must use those inherent traits of tenacity and self-belief along with their deep understanding of themselves and their business to make an educated best guess. In this case, a daring decision was made to stall growth within the business, for a short period, and take stock of the achievements thus far and potential future direction. As strong feeling of needing to protect what had already been developed and allow time to focus on the current and future needs of the business was certainly the deciding factor here.

Edward also chose to involve external consultancy, feeling that a fresh pair of competent eyes would aid him in this reflective process.

The choice of consultancy style was paramount to its success and Edward chose a non-traditional format, with high levels of challenge as well as support. Through this conversation he was able to redefine his business plan, re-evaluate the use and value of his own time and consider the detailed implementation of structure and process to both the operational management and financial administration of the company.

Lack of delegation of workload was recognized as a risk to the business and so a skills needs analysis was used to formulate job descriptions and aid in recruitment decisions. A cost–time analysis was also carried out, resulting in changes to management of company assets and alterations to geographic areas of work. Edward also developed a robust business contingency plan and set SMART targets surrounding growth and diversification. He continues to engage with external consultancy, from a variety of specialist sources, to help him better understand his business and its ever-changing complexities.

Two of the quite unintended side effects of this review were a change in the measures of success for the business and an improved work–life balance for Edward himself. The implementation of structure can seem, at the outset, constraining for many entrepreneurs, but, when it is correctly managed, with careful delegation and conscious consideration of advice available, it can offer direction and business improvement that tenacity and drive alone cannot. Needless to say the business has now re-entered growth and is moving forward at an even greater pace than before.

These are a couple of examples of how entrepreneurs have success-fully tackled the growth stage of their business. So how as a rule of thumb might the growth of your business develop?

Five key stages of growth for start-ups

As you will have read in the first chapter, only around 40 per cent of start-ups in the UK will continue trading after a five-year time frame. We suggest there are five key stages of growth that a new company will go through as it starts to scale up its business. Here is a checklist of what you need to be aware of and consider as you grow your company.

1 Know your product market fit

In which market sector does your product or service fit? What is the value you bring to the customer? How unique is your offering? This is your first area of focus. Don't get distracted. Prove your value and you will attract customers. Ask customers, family and friends to recommend you and create case studies. Give discounts to attract new business.

2 Building a solid customer base

Your reputation is growing. You have a growing customer base. Don't get distracted by only fulfilling orders. Spend at least 60 per cent of your time in this stage generating recurring and new sales. Your objective is to reduce the price discounts offered till now. You are moving from a part-time job into a full-time order-taking role.

3 Scaling up your business

Make your sales efforts more predictable. While referrals are still important you will want to use advertising to make your sales efforts and forecasting more predictable. You may have others on board but you may still feel overwhelmed. You are doing everything at once. This is often the most difficult stage.

4 Growth processes, procedures and tools

With growth and predictability improved, more clarified processes, procedures, systems and consistent training are an absolute must. Focus in designing job descriptions, clarifying each team member's responsibilities (and what they are not) and individual KPIs. Ensure

you improve your sales and forecasting techniques. An ob
here is to increase revenue per customer.

5 Introducing team members and ensuring your systems work

Scale up and fine tune your processes, procedures, systems and
consistent training. Ensure consistency by training all team members
how to use your processes and systems. Focus here on hiring new
members. Get your reporting systems to the standard you need to
continually grow. You should now start managing rather than being
involved in all operational activities.

Key tasks

- Are you ready to build your business? Have you thought through what structure to put in place to fully capitalize on your own strengths and weaknesses?

- Search on the web to find out about the range of analysis tools you might be able to utilize during the recruitment process.

- Have you talked to your current client/customer base to find out from them how they might contribute to the growth of your business?

- Think about how you are scaling up your business. Are you building a solid customer base that is not just reliant on price discounting?

- How good are your processes and procedures if you are starting to build a team?

03

The management side of building your business

Introduction

As an entrepreneur you need to be able not only to lead but also to manage. People often confuse management and leadership. What is the difference between the two?

- Leadership is evolutionary (future-oriented).
- Management is operational (present-oriented).

Management activities tend to be task-oriented and include things like day-to-day planning, budgeting, problem solving, administration and control. Leadership activities such as those above are less easily defined but can have more far-reaching future consequences. Do not think of leadership as more desirable than management. Rather, you should understand the differences and be capable of using both skill sets according to the situation.

Management is not just a set of behaviours that you apply the same way everywhere. Rather, it is the ability to assess an environment – and its people – and choose the right skills and applications for the specific situation. According to a Harvard study, 85 per cent of managers get ahead based on their ability to deal with people, while only 15 per cent do so based on technical competence, and the former is the focus of this chapter. Management is about getting results. Getting results means delivering your objectives, which should mean adding value and profitability to your organization.

Your management role and responsibilities

As you build your business, you will need to employ others. Let's look at a couple of different options and how your management role will differ in each of these situations. One approach as we have mentioned in the previous chapter could be to bring in specialist/senior managers who in turn will recruit others and become a self-directed team. This means that they would have their own budget, create their own product range or service offering, and be accountable for their teams output.

Option two would be for the entrepreneur to recruit a task-oriented operational team. Let's start by looking at the first option.

Managing the specialist/senior managers

We discussed in an earlier chapter the more holistic methodology that many entrepreneurs take towards recruitment and the management of skills and attitudes within start-up businesses. Managing the senior team is, in many ways, an extension of this approach. Your aim should be to foster a culture of autonomy and shared responsibility. This can be a tough balancing act between empowering the team to effectively lead their individual business area and ensuring that the overall vision for business success is achieved. There are some key concepts that can assist with this style of management:

- The specialist/senior manager would develop the strategic plan for their own area of work, linked directly to the overall business plan. They should also consider any areas where their plan will benefit, compete with or duplicate the work of other business areas. This will involve them interacting with their peer group and therefore create a much deeper understanding of the business as a whole and open communication between team members.

- You as the owner of the business plus your top team should recognize specialist knowledge and experience of both yourselves as well as others. Delegation of tasks should take place based upon who is best suited to perform them rather than on who is perceived as more senior or whose job it is perceived to be.

- In managing these senior managers, you should offer a high level of support and low level of instruction or direction. Healthy competition in this environment is a great motivator, but it is paramount to ensure that this does not become a barrier to the relationships between individuals.

- Competing viewpoints, challenge, and constructive action-based criticism should be welcomed. Disagreement between senior colleagues is not unusual and should not be swept under the carpet. Resolution by win–win style negotiation and clear contracting between colleagues will increase the overall strength of the team.

- When you get together with your senior managers, meetings should focus upon strategy, presentation of performance (positive and negative) and future plans. Blame and finger pointing should be actively discouraged. On occasions when this type of behaviour occurs it can be prudent to ask how the aggressor is planning to assist in resolution.

- Performance issues relating to individual senior managers should always be dealt with on a one-to-one basis, away from junior colleagues and the wider top team. Many entrepreneurs choose to use external sources of HR support in these instances to avoid negative effects occurring in the wider business.

Moving on to the second option, you grow your business by setting up and recruiting a task-oriented operational team. How should you manage this type of team?

Managing a task-oriented operational team

This team is going to directly report in to you. What do you need to do to start the ball rolling to get them to perform to the best of their potential?

Point your team in one direction

Teams need to know where they're going. Team members perform best when they unite with a keen sense of mission, knowing they're heading somewhere special. If the aiming point is clear and the vision is compelling, it draws the team together and pulls them forward. Concentrate on making the vision a cause. Teams get fired up about crusades and not about 'strategic plans'.

Give the team a sense of purpose that captures their imagination and encourages them to close ranks. Coordinate team effort by concretely explaining to the team the specific results the team is expected to achieve. You must believe in what the team is doing. If not, how can turn the vision into reality? True leaders, true visionaries, do everything to control events. True leaders are driven by a vision, every team member must be part of that vision, and that vision must encompass the individual visions of every team member. In addition, nothing leads to disillusionment more quickly if the team feels that it cannot change or implement what it is supposed to change. 'I have a dream!' was Martin Luther King's message. He certainly had a dream and by pulling out the essence and distilling it into a few clear, crisp paragraphs, he told everyone prepared to listen the essence of his dream. This dream was underpinned by a great, overarching simplicity: make Americans equal. Like most of the best visions, his was simple. Simplicity has the benefit of being easily communicated and remembered. Team visions, too, must be simple and describe what the team is supposed to achieve in the given time span.

Set a clear agenda

Team members need a clear sense of direction. How else can the team be effective? Clear priorities help team members to figure out how to spend their time. Create an action plan setting out the agenda with crystal clear tactical objectives giving the team laser-like focus. Keep objectives concrete and tie them to a specific timetable. Potential resistance can be defused when your instructions are unequivocal and easily understood. Make known your commitment to them and their commitment to achieving the goals known. Tell them at the outset that they can expect some mid-course corrections. The agenda will have to be adapted as the situation demands it. But, always keep it clear and communicate it constantly. Of course, key team members can contribute to designing the team's priorities and objectives. You must consider their input. That's real delegation. The more they can shape the agenda, the more buy-in and commitment they'll show. Their ideas might, also, dramatically improve your sense of priorities. In the final analysis, though, you remain responsible and accountable.

Set goals and targets

Goals need to be SMART – specific, measureable, achievable, realistic and timed.

There should be *strategic* business goals, for example:

'We are going to expand our product range and find new markets in the US by the end of this financial year.'

'We are going to increase our customer satisfaction rating given during feedback questionnaires circulated post completion of sale in the property sector from 45 per cent to 80 per cent by December 2018.'

Performance goals:

'Double our website traffic within the next 12 months by providing more comprehensive health care information to accompany the exercise regime that we have in place on our site.'

'Implement process improvements to help achieve 7 per cent uptime of equipment and quality of 98 per cent by April 2018'.

Operational goals:

'On an ongoing basis accurately process and despatch 98 per cent of our premium product range from our main warehouse within the one-week window we advertise on our website.'

'Conduct an educational programme to reduce customer returns from the assembly department by 15 per cent by December 2017.'

And of course *personal* goals:

> 'You should produce an advertising campaign to attract a minimum of 3,000 new purchasers by XYZ period of time.'

> 'You should develop your PowerPoint skills so that you can create the required visuals for two of our consultants who deliver ten days of training each to Unilever per month.'

Focus on results. Go for those operational improvements that are most urgently needed. Focus on those things that go straight to the bottom line or that contribute directly to competitive position. Stake out specific targets. Aim for a few – but ambitious – goals. Go for measurable gains.

Ensure roles and responsibilities are understood

Ensure team members know what you expect from them. Don't leave them to figure things out on their own. Get rid of role ambiguity. Nail down every team member's responsibilities with clarity, precision and attention to detail. There must be no question regarding where one job stops and the next one starts. Leave no blur regarding the responsibilities each team member is supposed to shoulder. Figure out precisely what needs to be done and who's going to do which part of it, and communicate your plan. Give every team member a brief job description. State your expectations regarding standards of performance. Describe the chain of command in the team. Outline each person's spending limits, decision-making authority, and reporting requirements.

Everyone will be best served if you put this information down in writing. Check to make sure that each team member understands the team's (whole) set-up and how it fits together. Be careful to avoid job overlap, since that feeds power struggles, wastes resources and frustrates those involved. When explaining to team members what to do also specify what they should not do. Differentiate between crucial tasks and peripheral, low-priority activities. Spell out what needs to be accomplished in each position and for what each team member will be held accountable. Once you have done this, pay attention to what team members are doing. Keep everyone on track. If you see something going wrong, fix it immediately.

Be urgent

Your role as a manager is to energize the team, mobilize it and keep change as it happens from choking off its energy. You need to show a strong sense of urgency. What do your work habits say to the team? What about your personal productivity? Does your behaviour show a burning job commitment? Without a sense of urgency you can't function as the pivotal influence around which the team can coalesce. Like it or not, you're the example that team members take their cue from.

Keep the pressure on for productivity. Inertia is your big enemy. Set tight deadlines. Push for quicker decisions. Operate with a bias for action. Let everybody know that you will be tolerant of honest mistakes, but intolerant of inaction and inertia. Praise those who are energetic. Nip at the heels of those who drag their feet. Instead of patiently planning and preparing, just get going. Move immediately to get results.

Confront reality

You must engineer individual efforts into a unified, coherent, collective team effort. You must create a team culture and team language relevant to the job in hand. After all, your reputation as a manger is at stake. The best way to protect that reputation is to get results.

Your team members and you undermine that credibility when you wallow or waffle. Don't confuse respect with popularity. Focus on results. Ensure you solicit other people's opinions. That positions you to wield authority in an informed manner. All team members have a voice, but you ultimately have the responsibility to ensure your team is efficient and productive (and profitable, if pertinent).

Set the standard

High-performance teams are disciplined. You must function as the main disciplinary agent. Start by setting high standards. Then defend them. Aim for excellence. Build pride. Keep things tightly organized. Don't allow team members to drift into old routines or habits. If you see a mistake, grasp the nettle and address it immediately. Hold team members accountable for all their assigned tasks. Keep them to their agreed timetables and deadlines. Don't be vague or fuzzy in laying down the rules, or in explaining what you want, or inconsistent in enforcing objectives. If you make as many exceptions as you do rules, you have no rules. Always be prepared to back up your words with action. Team members will listen to what you have to say, but their behaviour will be shaped by what you do. Remember that you have no more powerful way to communicate than by example.

Compliment and praise

Reward, reward and reward good performance. The intangible rewards you have to offer are limitless:

- words of encouragement compliments;
- empathy and understanding;
- a note of appreciation or a sincere thank you;
- stopping to share a coffee, or taking a team member to lunch;
- giving team members special assignments or more decision-making authority;
- asking about the family;
- celebrating small victories;
- soliciting opinions and suggestions;
- listening, really listening;
- a smile or a warm handshake or pat on the back;
- taking someone into your confidence;
- asking team members for help, which is gratifying because it validates their worth.

Caring takes time. It requires that you pay attention to what's happening. Create a supportive team environment – nurture – and watch it bring out the best in people. Show approval and see how it arms the team. When you affirm, you empower. People feel safer, valued and more optimistic. Trust levels increase. Team members are more creative and engage their talents more fully. If you make every member of the team feel special, you'll end up with a very special team.

Leaders must wake people out of inertia. They must get people excited about something they've never seen before, something that does not yet exist.

Rosabeth Moss Kanter

Know your team and ensure communication flows

You can't lead by example if the team can't see you. Knowing your team means engaging with them. Look for strengths. Weaker points. Aspirations and work preferences. Experience and areas of expertise. Concerns and points of resistance. The sharper your insights into each team member, the better the odds that you'll manage more effectively. Of course, team members are the cornerstones of team effort, so don't take anyone – especially your key people – for granted. Keep them. Ensure they're on board emotionally. The way to do this is to give the team constant updates. Even no news is news. If you don't regularly update the team, they'll fill in the blanks themselves and you feed the rumour mill by default. Unless you speak for yourself, somebody will speak for you. If you want certain information to stick, keep saying it. If you have to deliver a complex or difficult message, put it in writing. Since communication travels four times as fast from the top down as from the bottom up, you should put new 'pipelines' in place to carry information to you.

If you know what the problems are and hear about them early enough, it is usually possible to fix them. So deputize every team member. Ask them to go looking for problems. As well as looking for proof that changes are happening or working, also search for evidence of areas of activity where there needs to be improvement or remedial action taken. Bring your team together often. Talk. Air issues and discuss. Pool everyone's thoughts on how to resolve problems so as to keep everyone in the loop. Invite argument and allow conflict. You'll end up with better solutions. Don't allow differences to be swept under the rug as they will come back to haunt the team later. You won't have a high-performance team unless you meet the tough issues head on. Remember what Colin Powell said: 'The day soldiers stop bringing you their problems is the day you stop leading them. They have either lost confidence that you can help them or concluded that you do not care. Either case is a failure of leadership.'

The casting of people – determining who goes, who stays and who goes where – carries a lot of weight. Put people in the right place to begin with, and you won't be forced to make changes later. With new challenges rewrite job descriptions. Start from scratch in analysing your available people assets. Check for people's adaptability. Ask yourself who is best suited for which role. If you discover there are weak players that you must use, position them where they'll hurt the team least and eventually take appropriate action. Size up your team with a dispassionate, discerning eye. You can't afford to sit back and figure out your team members as the months go by. You need to make informed judgements immediately. If you don't trust your skills at this, or if you feel that you just can't make the time, get help.

Pay attention to process

High-performance teams always pay attention to process. This is your team's internal machinery of how it goes about its business. All managers should focus attention on process. What's going on inside the team? Analyse its effectiveness. Determine what's missing, what's getting in the way, what needs to change. Regularly stop the team in its tracks. Call a halt long enough to let the team hold a mirror up to itself. Process analysis is as simple as saying:

'Let's look at what's going on now.'

'How do you feel about that?'

'Let's analyse how we're working together as a team.'

CASE STUDY   Phaidon International

This London-based recruiter was founded back in 2005 by its Chief Executive, Adam Buck, and now 11 years later numbers 130 employees. In 2016 it scooped second place in the *Sunday Times* 100 Best Small Companies to Work For.

So how has this SME achieved such an accolade?

Starting with the hiring process they believe it is important to give an upper-quartile salary and good benefits to attract the right calibre of person so that ultimately they can promote from within. It's a youthful workforce with currently 60 per cent of employees aged between 21 and 25, and one of the benefits they can offer is the opportunity to work in their offices overseas in New York, San Francisco, Singapore, Hong Kong and Zurich. Once they have offered a role within the company they make sure that that person is well versed in the company's mission, vision and values by sending them a brochure entitled *Phaidon at a Glance*. During induction they show a video covering their purpose, ambition, core principles and ethos.

This is followed by a Myers Briggs assessment, and a bespoke training programme spread over a 12-week period, which primarily involves training on the job, coaching and mentoring. To underpin this learning during monthly business reviews and assessments for promotion employees are asked to explain how they regularly demonstrate ability, loyalty and character. A monthly newsletter highlights high achievers who demonstrate these characteristics and they are invited to attend lunch club rewards, senior management away days and the AGM to further launch a new mission statement.

In scoring terms employees gave 'experience here is valuable for the future' 96 per cent, 'prospects within the company are positive' 97 per cent, and 'satisfaction with pay and benefits' 94 per cent. This speaks for itself!

Emotional intelligence

What we haven't looked at so far is how to work with people's feelings and emotions and self-worth. This involves using 'invisible' skills. As a manager you can't ignore this part of your exchange with others.

You need to build trusting relationships in order to achieve targets, get people to think creatively and take the initiative without feeling that they are going to be blamed if things don't go to plan. The working world is much messier and more complex now, and the need for speed of change and reaction to the marketplace is key to a company's survival. All of this means that people need to be far more resilient under pressure, and confident enough to self-manage and take the initiative.

We have always known that feelings and emotions are powerful drivers, but it was Daniel Goleman who coined the term 'emotional intelligence' in his research, first published in 1995 in his book *Emotional Intelligence: Why it can matter more than IQ.* Emotional intelligence, unlike mental intelligence, focuses on understanding our emotions and feelings and those of others. We all have times when we feel anxieties, are irritable or depressed. Goleman states that if we have emotional self-control in these situations we can have the capacity to bounce back far more quickly from life's

Figure 3.1   The visible and invisible skills of a manager

Technical Skills	Generic Skills	Team Skills	Emotional Skills
'Visible Skills' ⟶			'Invisible Skills'
Job skills	Time management	Collaboration	Empathy
	Problem solving	Communication	Self-awareness
	Setting priorities	Negotiation	Social awareness

setbacks and upsets. Having the capacity to notice and control our feelings can act as a steering method in our lives, and enables us to have a surer sense of how we really feel about personal decisions, from whom to marry to what job to take. Self-motivation, self-control and being able to 'get into the flow' is another key element in emotional intelligence, and can result in people being far more focused and productive. Being self-motivated can put you in a position where you can enjoy work for its own sake, without looking for extrinsic reward.

Leading on from this is optimism, which does not mean being unrealistically positive all the time. It does, however, determine how a person deals with setbacks. When things don't quite go to plan emotionally intelligent managers deal with setbacks or adversity and stay motivated. It's not the situation that's the issue; it's the way that you respond. Being optimistic and having self-confidence means that you cope well with frequent frustration and stress. As Winston Churchill said, 'Success consists of going from failure to failure without loss of enthusiasm.'

All these skills, strengths and attitudes come from within ourselves – we call these elements the intrapersonal core capabilities. This approach is not just about being inward looking. Having emotional intelligence also means being able to recognize emotions in others, having empathy and seeing things from the other person's point of view. In other words, having interpersonal core capabilities. In the business world this is a very important characteristic, and is the guiding light for any star business developer. Now you don't have to be a business developer to use this skill. As a manager you also need to be able to empathize and build trusting relationships with your co-workers. The term 'manager' automatically means other people are involved – be it members of your team, or internal customers. Being able to see things from another person's perspective gives us the capacity to get our ideas accepted, since we can also take into account the needs of the other person.

Influencing others and 'selling' our ideas is one of the most powerful attributes of leadership. Empathy is also of importance during group decision-making activities. If you are facilitating the group, you can understand and take into account other people's views, and so move more rapidly to an agreed outcome. So remember:

- Team problems are often *emotional* rather than factual.
- People quit their job, do not perform at their best, or resist change for *emotional* reasons.
- Companies lose customers for *emotional* reasons.
- Companies hire the wrong people because they focus more on their professional than *emotional* and social skills.
- Companies suffer big losses or die because they focus on bottom-line results and forget the *emotions* and motivation of their employees.
- Managers fail because they are not *emotionally* intelligent.

Delegation

Delegation requires you as a manager to be strong, supportive and resilient. If all goes well, your team members should get the credit. If it goes wrong, the manager accepts responsibility and is accountable. This is fair, since the manager is ultimately responsible for assessing any given situation – including the risks entailed – and in turn the level of freedom that can safely be granted to team members to deal with it.

Figure 3.2 The level of increased involvement

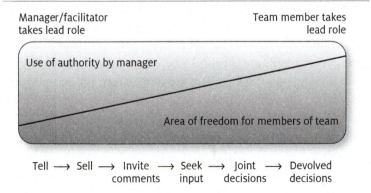

Manager/facilitator takes lead role · Team member takes lead role

Use of authority by manager

Area of freedom for members of team

Tell ⟶ Sell ⟶ Invite comments ⟶ Seek input ⟶ Joint decisions ⟶ Devolved decisions

If a team is relatively inexperienced, then more guidance is req
As you will see in level 1 below the manager makes all the deci
The aim with delegation is to rarely use this level, and move up the
numerical scale below as quickly as possible.

Different levels of delegation and enablement / empowerment

The manager:

1 **decides and announces the decision (*tells*):** The manager
   reviews options in terms of objectives, priorities, timescale, etc,
   then decides the action and informs the team of the decision.
   The team plays no active part in making the decision. The team
   may grumble that the manager has not considered their input or
   welfare but, since this is a task-based decision, so be it.

2 **decides and then communicates the decision (*sells*):** The
   manager makes the decision as in 1 above, and then explains
   reasons for the decision, particularly the positive benefits that the
   team, customers or the organization will enjoy from it. This way,
   the manager is seen by the team to recognize the team's importance, and to have some concern for the team.

3 **presents the decision with background ideas (*invites comments
   or questions*):** The manager presents the decision along with
   some of the background that led to the decision. Team members
   are invited to ask questions and discuss the rationale behind the
   decision. This enables them to understand and accept or agree
   with the decision more easily than in 1 and 2 above. This more
   participative and engaging approach enables the team to appreci-
   ate the issues and reasons for the decision, and the implications of
   all the options. This has a more motivational approach than 1 or
   2 because of the higher level of team involvement and discussion.

4 **suggests a provisional decision and invites discussion about
   it (*seeks input*):** The manager discusses and reviews the provisional decision with the team on the basis that the manager will

take their views on board before making the final decision. This way, team members have some real influence over the manager's final decision. This acknowledges that the team has something to contribute to the decision-making process, which is more involving and more motivational than level 3.

5 **presents the situation, gets suggestions, then decides (*joint decision*):** The manager presents the situation, and maybe some options, to the team. Team members are encouraged and expected to offer ideas and additional options, and discuss implications of each possible course of action. The manager then decides the best option to take. This level is one of high and specific involvement for the team, and is appropriate particularly when the team has more detailed knowledge or experience than the manager. Being high-involvement and high-influence for the team this level provides more motivation and freedom than any previous level.

6 **explains the situation, defines the parameters and asks the team to decide (*devolved decision*):** At this level the manager has effectively delegated responsibility for the decision to the team, albeit within the manager's stated limits. The manager may or may not choose to be a part of the team that decides. While this level appears to gives a huge responsibility to the team, the manager can control the risk and outcomes to an extent, according to the constraints that they stipulate. This level is more motivational than any previous one, and requires a mature team.

7 **allows the team to identify the problem, develop the options and decide on the action, within the manager's received limits (*devolved decision*):** This is obviously an extreme level of freedom, whereby the team is effectively doing what the manager did in level 1. Team members are given responsibility for identifying and analysing the situation, the process for resolving it, developing and assessing options, evaluating implications, and then deciding on and implementing their preferred

course of action. The manager also states in advance that they will support the decision and help the team implement it. The manager may or may not be part of the team, and if so then has no more authority than anyone else. This level is potentially the most motivational of all, but also potentially the most disastrous. Not surprisingly the team must be mature and competent, and capable of acting at what is a genuinely strategic decision-making level.

Summary checklist

In summary, the manager's role and responsibilities in creating a motivational task-oriented team environment includes:

1 **Being holistic:** Are things outside the team helping or hindering performance? What about policies, strategies, structures, and the market?

2 **Goals:** Do team members understand and accept the team's primary task?

3 **Roles:** What do team members expect of one another? Are these expectations clear and acceptable? How are conflicts handled? Is unnecessary duplication avoided? Who does what?

4 **Processes:** How does information flow and the need for coordination handled? How are problems solved, decisions made and adhered to? Are reporting procedures clear and concise?

5 **Relationships:** How do members treat and feel about each other? To learn what they think about you complete the exercise below. Are team members' needs for recognition, support and respect adequately met? Is there effective analysis and feedback of group and individual performance?

Exercise   ## Questions for personal feedback

Use these questions (or write your own) to ask team members for feedback on things you want to find out about yourself.

Do you see me as someone who…

1 offers constructive evaluation as needed?

2   encourages original ideas?

3 expresses ideas clearly and concisely?

4 provides good summaries on an issue when needed?

5 contributes without cutting off others?

6   helps to get to the crux of the matter?

7 provides helpful, objective feedback to others?

8 listens with understanding to what others say?

9   helps members express their ideas?

10 gives good suggestions on how to proceed?

11   encourages a group to high levels of productivity?

12 senses when to talk and when to listen?

13 makes others feel at ease?

14 helps a team to stay on target?

15 likes people?

16 yields to team pressures?

17 annoys others?

18 sticks blindly to the point?

19 is hard to understand?

20 runs away when faced with a problem?

21 makes unjustifed assumptions?

22 fights rather than works?

23 blocks the team?

24 likes to wander?

25 dominates and imposes their will on the team?

26 is judgemental?

Key tasks

- Review your relationship with your specialist/senior managers. Are you fully utilizing their expertise? Do they need any more support from you? Ask them!

- Think through how holistic you currently are as a manager, and change or improve where necessary.

- Assess where you might enable and empower and delegate more.

- Expand your knowledge of emotional intelligence. You will find books that are currently available on this topic in the reference list at the back of the book.

04

Recruiting talent

Introduction

So you're ready to build your business and bring on board your top team. Recruitment agencies and job boards are a given approach, but internet sourcing using social and professional networks such as LinkedIn and BeKnown are becoming the sourcing tools for hiring hard to find talent. By performing key word searches you can gain access to the same candidates previously held only by established recruitment agencies. Goggle+ is currently underused, but by its relative newness it has the advantage of holding up-to-date profiles of candidates.

And of course there is word-of-mouth recommendations. This is where it is important for you to be involved in networking with key decision makers from a cross-section of industries. When you are looking to recruit at a senior level remember degrees are only half the story. Experience and attitude are often more important and you must determine which is right for your start-up. Connect with your sector professional bodies to give you plenty of opportunities to go to events, attend sector specific conferences, or to network. In these environments you will not only get the opportunity to promote your start-up, but also hear and find talent for you to recruit.

Some personality testing resources, including assessment instruments, are available free on the internet or at relatively low cost from appropriate providers, and they are wonderful tools for self-awareness, personal development, working with people and for helping to develop better working relationships. Some instruments however are rather more expensive, given that the developers and psychometrics organizations need to recover their development costs. For this reason, scientifically validated personality testing instruments are rarely free. The free tests that are scientifically validated tend to be 'lite' introductory instruments which give a broad indication rather than a detailed analysis. Do seek appropriate training and accreditation if you wish to pursue and use psychometrics testing in a formal way within your company.

Referring to Chapter 2 and the Myers Briggs Type Indicator (MBTI), we mentioned the concept of perceiving and judging. We just want to highlight the importance of this during recruitment for the entrepreneur.

Perceiving individuals prefer a flexible and spontaneous way of life. They like to understand and adapt to the world rather than organize it. Others may see this person as open to new experiences and information. Do you recognize this in yourself? Your job as a company owner is to ensure you have a balanced team around you.

You might be great at formulating new ideas and concepts but not so good at other aspects of running your business. Judging individuals, according to Myers Briggs, prefer a planned or orderly way of life, like to have things settled and organized, feel more comfortable when decisions are made, and like to bring life under control as much as possible. Do you need this 'balance' in your company?

The three-tier recruitment process

During the recruitment process you could use a three-tier process that a lot of employers are now adopting:

1 Job description (tasks, responsibilities and line reports)

2 Candidate competencies (skills, experience, education)

3 Person specification (attitudes, personality traits, wider team/ business requirements and values)

With regard to person specification my management consultant colleague Mary Reggie De Silva from Kuala Lumpur suggests that

a behavioural competency framework (see the box) could
to select the best talent.

Competency-based recruitment

Here are some competencies to look out for that give rise
to superior job performance across any entrepreneurial,
professional, technical or managerial roles.

1 **Helping and service competencies** revolve around those who
   are sensitive to their surroundings and are very sharp-eyed
   while having a hands-on approach in their work. They have the
   desire to serve others by observing their needs which are often
   not expressed verbally, but which are noticed through their
   actions and feelings.

2 **Achievement and action competencies** are in people who
   have the ability to make improvements or who can create
   opportunities merely by setting up a clear and orderly system.
   They sense that something can be done through specific action
   and will go all out to the bottom of issues to find a solution.

3 **Influencing competencies** are powerful as one has the ability
   to influence, impress or have an impact on others by creating
   positive dynamics within the organization. They have the ability
   to draw people towards their ideas and philosophies.

4 **Personal effectiveness competencies** provide the commanding
   ability of being very calm and stable during stressful situations.
   They are not shaken in crisis and are able to turn on the
   situation to develop a comfortable pace to move forward.

5 **Managerial competencies** are in people who have resilient
   leadership qualities and they have the aptitude of having an
   impact on others due to their influential nature. They are often
   able to recognize and inspire the need for self-development in
   others.

6 **Cognitive competencies** are recognized in people who have conceptual and critical thinking abilities and therefore are able to evaluate situations with the purpose of providing solutions to problems in a logical way. They are usually specialists in their own field and have a wide range of technical and work experience.

While recruitment and selection are always perceived as bringing in new blood into the organization give thought to identify suitable candidates from within the company. Any job is unlikely to require all the competencies. Having fewer competencies allow the selection process to be manageable while it must be agreed that some competencies take a longer time to train and develop than others.

As an alternative to an interview, candidates can be asked to rate their competencies through a self-descriptive questionnaire, with statement such as:

- I am good at analysing situations before making a conclusion.
- I am able to identify issues faced by others by being more observant.
- I am a calm person irrespective of the situation.
- I am usually able to persuade people to see things my way.
- I am good at recognizing the weaknesses of others and have good mentoring abilities.

C E Bethel-Fox
Based on *Competency Models and the Public Service of Malaysia*

We would suggests that the interview questions should related to the job requirements (competencies) in the job description. Questions on the candidate's career history are useful but should be kept to a minimum. This is past history. What you need to know and should base your questioning on relates to future potential, getting candidates to explain and demonstrate their ability to perform the role being applied for.

Interview preparation stage

With regard to the job description, start by thinking about the key skills, competencies and other considerations that you are looking for in the applicants' CVs. This will allow you to properly screen CVs and prepare the appropriate questions to ask during any interview session.

Use the job and candidate requirements in order to prepare specific questions to ask an applicant if there have been any gaps identified when screening their CV.

Remember that qualifications, education, country experience and languages are objective. The more candidates that satisfy these, the more important it is to uncover additional evidence based on your prepared questions.

Identifying job and candidate requirements serve as a guide for scoring/evaluating CVs. This is the primary instrument of recruitment. The more specific its definition, the better your time and energy will be applied in the selection process.

Define the job description

The job description helps you to understand exactly why you are recruiting and what you are looking for. The more specific the job description, the easier it will be to find a good candidate. Defining the job description is not simply a bureaucratic exercise. It is an essential part of recruitment. This responsibility is the hiring manager's and not the HR department's.

Define the job requirements

Ensure the essential *job requirements* are incorporated in the job description:

- job description responsibilities and deliverables;
- experience (including experience of a particular country if required);
- education and qualifications;
- languages spoken;
- activities that must be done, or up and coming special projects you are planning.

Define the candidate's skills, competencies and attributes

Make sure the essential candidate *skills, competencies and attributes* for this job are incorporated in the job description.

- A *skill* is the capacity to successfully accomplish something requiring special knowledge or ability. Examples include: type 70 words per minute, or speak Russian.
- A *competence* can be described as 'an underlying characteristic of a person which results in effective and/or superior performance in a role'. Examples include: achieve results or provide direction.
- An *attribute* is a quality or characteristic that a person is born with. Examples include: highly strung, tolerant, etc.

Determine screening and assessing criteria

The criteria used to screen and accept or reject CVs are based on the job and candidate requirements listed in the job description under 'Essential skills, experience and qualifications' and 'Competencies and personal attributes'.

- Determine *screening criteria* – what are essential job and candidate requirements you must identify to screen CVs?
- Determine *assessing criteria* – what questions must you prepare to probe and clarify whether essential job and candidate requirements mentioned in the CV are valid?

If a candidate does not possess all the screening criteria *but* is working to achieve these (for example, has not yet completed a particular qualification) and *seems* to possess the competencies and personal attributes required (team player/self motivated, etc), you may decide to interview them.

CV screening – the telltale signs

- Has there been a lot of job hopping? If yes, is the candidate right for the post advertised?
- Check out for gaps in employment, eg 2007–2009 could be 12/07 to 1/09 – just over a year!
- Language – is the CV full of management speak, or bland generic words not revealing personality or originality of thought?
- Layout – is the CV layout tidy and accurate, suggesting attention to detail, or crammed together copy that might suggest a chaotic mind?
- Achievement – is the result described concretely, detailing what exactly was done? Any achievements that are listed without also showing the improvements or changes – quantified in £/$, or % – are useless.

In preparation for the interview, depending on the size of your company it is best to involve all stakeholders during the interview process, so a panel is advisable. You should create a list of agreed questions that you will ask in turn. Each candidate needs to have the same questions asked of them for equal opportunity purposes. Probably around five questions is sufficient, and make sure the questions are open – in other words, they cannot be answered just by a 'yes' or 'no'. The interview session would be a little short otherwise! You should use questions in general and specifically biographical and competency questions related to your team's key result areas. You must think through how each question is formulated, and understand the results you are looking to achieve. Talk with your HR department to clarify what questions you must *not* ask to stay within legal, diversity or ethical best-practice norms.

Carrying out the interview itself

Since you want to optimize the time you spend undertaking the interview, you should aim to relax the candidate as soon as possible, so that you can get them to 'open up' and explore factors that are important to the job.

Get the environment right. If it is going to be a one-to-one interview in your office, ensure privacy and no interruptions. Remember to turn off your mobile phone. Clear your desk as much as possible, keeping just the documents you require for the interview. This shows you are prepared and organized, and shows respect for the situation and the person you are interviewing. A desk will be a barrier, so arrange seating in an informal and relaxed way. If the interview session is to be with a panel, a meeting room would be best, ideally with a round table.

Use the interview to build rapport and create a positive image of your organization. The first minutes are crucial in setting the tone of the interview. So let's look at the interview in overview terms to start off with. A good way to open up the interview is to ask the candidate, 'What do you know about our organization?' It is surprising how many candidates don't even bother to check the organization's website for basics information about the company. It is not a very promising sign if they have not done at least this basic research prior to coming to the interview.

You can then progress to clarifying clearly and precisely big-picture information about the organization (not too much detail here – the candidate does not need to know about every department/product range; you want the time to be spent with them talking, not you). Then quickly move on to talk about your team, and the role that the applicant has applied for.

Use 'How' and 'What' questions wherever possible, and minimize the use of 'Why' as this can put pressure on the applicant as it suggests justification or defence is required. Since you want them to be relaxed, if you need to use 'Why' it is best used towards the end of an interview.

If a psychometric instrument has been used prior to the face-to-face interview, you will need to give feedback from the results. Position the test as a helpful guide for all parties, not the deciding factor.

Throughout the interview use open questions.

Control the interview by active listening. Take notes and ask probing questions that help you to understand exactly what the candidate did in previous roles.

Time should always be left for the candidate to ask questions themselves. This is where you get a real feeling about them as a person. What is important to them? How much do they understand about the roles and responsibilities of the post they are applying for?

End the interview positively by explaining the next steps and what will happen and by when.

Various interview questioning techniques

Open questions

Use 'open' (who, what, where, why, when, how, which) questions to open up the discussion. Open questions allow candidates to describe events from their own point of view. Examples include:

'What did you like best about your last position?'

'How do you see your career developing?'

'What attracted you to apply for this post?'

Closed questions

Closed questions start with a verb, 'Did you...?', 'Have you...?', 'Will you...?' They only require yes/no answers. These tend to close down conversation. Closed questions can be used to check facts or verify answers. Examples include:

'Did you succeed doing that?'

'Did you say that you worked in a marketing department for three years?'

'Have you more information to add?'

'Do you consider the projects you were involved in too regional?'

Biographical questions

Biographical questions relate to *past* jobs, life experiences and education that have helped the candidate to excel (competence) in their career. Examples include:

'What have you learned about your strengths as a result of working at the various jobs you have held?'

'What do you think you learnt working as an assistant manager?'

'How do you think your work experience and education will assist in this role?'

The benefit of using these questions to interviewers is that they reveal life and relevant work experiences and education required in various roles. These questions are used to get candidates to describe, in detail, the relevance of past positions to future roles and their responsibilities.

Competency questions

Competency questions describe 'how well a job is performed' or are used to describe what excellent performance should look like in a job. A competency is a fairly deep and enduring part of a person's personality and can predict behaviours and performance required to successfully meet the job tasks and responsibilities. These questions are used to get candidates to describe, in detail, the behaviours, skills and attributes required to meet job tasks and responsibilities in the role you have in mind. Examples include:

'How do you make sure that services you deliver meet customer needs fully?'

'Tell me about a demanding goal you set for yourself.'

'Tell me about a time when you have really had to dig deep to find out about an underlying problem.'

Probing questions

Remember to follow up on answers given. Whilst the wording of the opening question is vital, follow up questions are essential to allow you to probe deeper. We probe until it is clear what the candidate actually did. Never allow candidates to get away with generalizations. This is one of the most frequent errors made in interviews. Probing for full and accurate information requires skill and the interviewer's perseverance if certain areas of information are being avoided by the candidate. Examples include:

'Tell me more about it.'

'Can you think of another example where...?'

'What happened...? What was the outcome...?'

'What did you actually do or say?'

Leading questions

Avoid leading questions. These types of questions imply a particular answer is correct and so lead the candidate to give the reply s/he thinks you want to hear. For example, a poor leading question might be:

'We seek proactive people. How would you describe yourself – proactive or reactive?'

Double or multiple questions

Avoid double or multiple questions. With multiple questions, there is a tendency for the candidate to only answer one part of the question. For example:

'What is it that you enjoy most when working with people – having staff to manage or the challenge of motivating them?'

It would be must better to ask:

'What do you enjoy most when working with people?'

Theoretical questions

Avoid theoretical questions. You should be more interested in knowing what a candidate *would* do faced with the real situation, rather than if they know what they 'should' do. Therefore you want to seek out examples of what the candidate has actually done when faced with that situation. For example:

> 'Sometimes we give feedback and it is taken in the wrong way. What would you do if this were to happen to you?'

It is better to ask:

> 'Sometimes we give feedback and it is taken in the wrong way. What have you done in the past to ensure that your feedback is understood in the manner you meant it?'

Reliability of evidence

Encourage and facilitate potentially negative answers. Phrase questions to enable potentially negative answers to be given more readily. For example:

> 'We all have to lower our personal standards sometime. Can you tell me when you have had to compromise in this way?'

Ask questions that cover several situations to build up reliability. For example:

> 'We all have to lower our personal standards sometime. Can you tell me when you have had to compromise in this way in the office and with a client?'

Asking questions related to the candidate's CV

One section in a CV can be a mine of information. For example, under 'Sample Achievements' a candidate's CV states:

> 'I managed my team's capability development to embed the new OD and business processes, which raised the professional standing of the department with our customers. This included

team building, through coaching, support and the use of challenge techniques.'

Related questions you might ask here are:

'How did you actually manage this?'

'How many people were in your team?'

'What did "capability development" actually mean in this instance?'

'You say that you raised the team's professional standing. How did you measure this?'

'Give me three examples of "challenge techniques" you used.'

Questions you should never ask

In every job interview, the goal is to obtain important information while building a friendly rapport with the candidate. But some questions are just a little *too* risky. Protect yourself and your organization from legal trouble and embarrassment by avoiding the wrong questions while still getting to the root of the concern behind the question. Do not discriminate. We must *never* ask questions – this is a legal requirement – that may be thought to discriminate against a person's sex, sexual orientation, age, race, religion, marital status, pregnancy, disability, political views, etc. Also, stay away from making personal comments or statements during interviews. Candidates know their rights and will judge the interviewer and your company.

Look at the sample interview questions in Figure 4.1. You will see what is considered acceptable and unacceptable to ask, with a brief explanation below explaining the rationale. It is important to know how to turn possibly litigious questions into harmless, legal alternatives.

Why are some of the questions in Figure 4.1 unacceptable?

Question 1: Although this seems like the simplest and most direct way to find out if an candidate is legally able to work for your organization, it's not acceptable. Rather than enquiring about

citizenship, question whether or not the candidate is author-ized for work.

Question 3: You may want to know about religious practices to find out about weekend or other work schedules, but it's imperative that you refrain from asking directly about a candi-date's beliefs. Instead, just ask directly when they're able to work, and there will be no confusion.

Question 5: This question is too revealing of political and reli-gious affiliations that candidates are not required to share such information with potential employers. Additionally, this question has little to no relation to a candidate's ability to do a job. Ensure that your wording focuses on work.

Question 7: While maturity is essential for most positions, it's important that you don't make assumptions about a candi-date's maturity based on age. Equally, you have to be careful about discrimination towards applicants nearing retirement. Knowledge of an applicant's age can set you up for discrim-ination troubles down the road. To be safe, just ensure that the candidate is legally old enough to work for your organization.

Question 9: Clearly, the concern here is that family obligations will get in the way of work hours. Instead of asking about or making assumptions on family situations, get to the root of the issue by asking directly about the candidate's availability.

Question 11: The practice of inter-office relationships can be distracting, break up teams and cause a number of other problems in the workplace. But asking this question makes assumptions about the candidate's marital status and may even be interpreted as a come-on.

Check hobbies

We can identify what's really important to the candidate by know-ing what really *motivates* him or her. People's motivations relate to our values. If we can discover these it may allow us to find out

Figure 4.1 Acceptable or unacceptable questions

Which of the following are acceptable or unacceptable?	Acceptable?	Unacceptable?
1 Are you an EU citizen?		X
2 Are you authorized to work in the UK?	X	
3 Which religious holidays do you observe?		X
4 Are you always able to work within our required working week?	X	
5 Do you belong to a club or social organization?		X
6 Are you a member of a professional or trade group that is relevant to our industry?	X	
7 How old are you?		X
8 Are you over the age of 18?	X	
9 Do you have or plan to have children?		X
10 Can you get a babysitter on short notice for overtime or travel?	X	
11 What do you think of inter-office relationships?		X
12 Have you ever been disciplined for your behaviour at work?	X	

what candidates may be prepared to commit to. Bear in mind, the qualities you are looking for in a candidate depend on the job description.

Sailing example:

'What are you looking for when you go sailing?'

Answer 1: Getting away, being alone, thinking, forgetting, planning...

Answer 2: Finding a common focus of interest with friends, teamwork, forgetting the hierarchy...

Free time example:

'What do you do in your free time?'

Answer 1: Spend time with my family, watch TV...

Answer 2: Meet friends, manage a sports team...

After the interview

You will need to write up the hard evidence you observed during the interview and give detailed written feedback to HR (if you have an HR department) or others to allow them to inform candidates of how well they did. Candidates often request feedback, particularly if they work in-house already.

Finally, remember that the costs of one recruitment error can be enormous. I always ask myself 'Would I enjoy working with this person?' and 'What value will this person add to the business?' If there's any doubt I always say 'No'.

Tips and techniques

Summary of top 11 recruitment pitfalls

1 Failing to look for a candidate in-house.

2 Looking for an exact personal replica, 'mirror' or superhero.

3 Not explaining the process or next steps and when they will happen.

4 Going it alone – not involving HR or key stakeholders.

5 'Winging it', leading to a poor interview structure and using the wrong questions.

6 Going with 'gut feel' or 'first impressions'.

7 Missing signals.

8 The candidate not talking. The candidate should talk for 70 per cent of the interview at least.

9 Poor follow-up/selection process takes too long.

10 Over-promising, under-delivering.

11 Lack of professionalism.

Induction

When we go into organizations to do research we find that the induction process for new hires can often be quite skimpy. The aim of induction is to help new employees make a smooth, positive adjustment to your workplace. Induction must be designed to assist managers in providing new employees with valuable information about their organization and their new job.

The aim of induction is to:

- support your organization's business objectives through swift and effective introduction of personnel into their new position;
- reduce anxiety often experienced by changing job/organization;
- foster a positive attitude towards your organization;
- answer questions not handled at the time of recruitment;
- reinforce or establish realistic job expectations;
- through the provision of information and a well-planned induction programme, increase knowledge of the organization and the job, and so develop the confidence and motivation of all new staff.

What is your responsibility as a manager?

- Provide the new team member with a positive role model;
- provide specific information about the team and/or department structure:
  - organization and structure;
  - operational activities;
  - relationship of function to other teams or departments;
  - goals and current priorities;
  - introduce the new person to the team and job;
  - detailed explanation of job description;
- coordinate and individualize the induction activities;
- reinforce the new team member's introduction to your organization;
- make sure you are available and accessible during the first few days and weeks.

Why is proper induction so important?

First impressions last. When a new person joins the team, it is very important that they have a good impression of the organization itself and of you as the manager, and see how professionally and efficiently the team itself operates, as this will affect their attitude to working with you and the team.

They will also need very practical tools and equipment to do their job, so that they are able to make a positive contribution to your team immediately. Saying this might seem glaringly obvious, but I know from experience that a new person can often be squeezed into a space that is inappropriate for their requirements. I have seen sales staff who are on the telephone all day being put next to photo-copying machines; a new hire being put into an enclosed storeroom area with no natural light, and, of course, the three-legged table, with the fourth leg being propped up with phone directories! So, in practical terms what should you consider?

Prior to a new team member starting, and their first day

1 Organize desk/office and appropriate equipment and supplies:

  - mobile telephone;
  - e-mail access;
  - access to your organization's intranet and websites;
  - business cards;
  - laptop and appropriate software.

2 Prepare (with relevant personnel) their personal induction pack or employee handbook, which should include a copy of their job description and all contractual terms and conditions.

3 Agree with your HR or relevant personnel, within the first three days of the new team member joining your organization, when the new person should meet with them to go through your organization's employment practices and benefits. (This could be you on your own, of course, if you are a sole trader.)

4 Arrange a mentor or 'buddy' to help guide him/her through their first weeks in the organization and to answer any questions they may have. The 'buddy' can give a tour of the organization's facilities, to include:

  - rest rooms;
  - telephone/message systems;
  - mail room;
  - copy/fax machine;
  - conference rooms;
  - systems support;
  - equipment/supplies;
  - computers/printers;
  - storage/files;
  - books/references;

- kitchen and bulletin board;
- shopping facilities;
- parking.

5 End the new person's first day with a personal wrap-up to answer questions and make them feel at ease. At this time, it's a good idea to agree a date for an initial welcome lunch within the first two weeks.

Day 2 or 3

Once the new hire successfully ends his/her first day, your responsibility for providing job orientation isn't over – in fact it has just begun. Early in the first week you will need to devise a specific orientation plan. This induction plan is one that you work out directly with the person concerned to meet his/her individual needs.

To help you devise an effective, individualized induction plan consider the points and questions below:

- Early on during the first week, most likely the morning of day two, sit down with the new team member for about one hour to plan and agree with them the activities and goals for that week.
- Does the new person understand the team's goals as well as their specific job details?
- What do he/she need to know by the end of the first week?
- What experiences from this person's first day need reinforcement?
- Recall the wrap-up at the end of the first day and think about what the new team member may not have absorbed or may have had concerns about.
- What key policies and procedures do you need to convey during the first week? Those items critical to this person's job success are best handled now.
- What positive behaviours do you want to reinforce during this first week?

- What should you do to help integrate this person into his/her particular work group?

- How can you give this new person a sense of accomplishment during the first week? Prepare a list of specific work assignments that offer a rewarding experience for them.

- What feedback will they need from you?

- How can you make yourself accessible? The hours you are able to invest during this first week may save you hundreds of hours in the months to come. Assess what you need to do with the new team member, estimate how long it will take, schedule the activity and then commit yourself to carrying it out.

- Plan also to meet again at the end of the week or the start of week two for a review meeting. This review meeting enables you and the new team member to review the orientation plan and check off the items achieved. This process visibly confirms the person's accomplishments and progress. During the first month of employment, meet with him/her on a weekly basis.

After one month in the organization

View a new team member's orientation and training as a continuous process rather than as a single event. Many induction programmes I was involved with lasted up to one year. Your task as a manager is to provide all the information and tools they need to work effectively and productively.

Induction questions for managers to ask themselves after one month

Before the end of their first month, provide the new team member with additional details about their role in the immediate work group, department and division. In addition, be sure to provide the new team member with more information about their specific job. The following list of questions will help you clarify what should go into the evolving orientation plan for a new employee.

- What policies and procedures could affect this person's job performance? Does he/she understand all policies and procedures?

- What impressions or values do I want to reinforce to him/her?

- What specific tasks can I assign to him/her that will allow for growth? Examine all the tasks performed by people in the immediate work group, and structure the simpler ones into interesting and challenging assignments for the new person.

- What can you do to broaden your delegation of authority and decision making? Concentrate on getting specific tasks done, and increasingly delegate to the new team member as appropriate.

- What training objectives do you want to meet within the team member's first 3–6 months?

Hold a review session after one month. See sample questions in the box.

 Example   **Induction questionnaire at the end of the first month**

Name:
Please answer the following questions in writing and bring them with you to our meeting, scheduled for…

1   What were your ambitions when you started with us and how, if at all, have these changed?

2   What have you found satisfying about your work in this first month?

3   Is the work you are doing in line with the job description and position you were recruited for?

4   What kind of difficulty, if any, have you had in positioning yourself in the organization?

5 What specific assistance should I and the company give you in the next month(s) to make you still more effective?

6 What are you going to do to increase your professional efficiency in the next month(s)? [Get them to specify this.]

7 What are your suggestions for improving the way we induct new employees?

When your team member is six months in the organization

The following questions can help you to check if the first six months of orientation and training of your new team member was effective. These questions are just for you and can help you ensure that any future new team members get the best possible welcome into your team.

- What additional information would have helped my new team member during their first six months? Refer to your organization's employee handbook for relevant items not previously covered. For example, they may need to know about safeguarding confidential information.

- What additional policies and procedures does your team member need to better understand or have reinforced?

- What more can you do to reduce the time needed to manage this person? There are many learning experiences, such as working with a more experienced member of the team, that might help.

- How can you broaden your new team member's assignments so that they are continually challenged? The team member will experience growth in performing their job, and you need to match that growth with broader assignments.

- What feedback should you give on your new team member's performance? If you meet regularly with them and monitor their progress on their orientation plan, you may already be providing some feedback on their performance. You may also consider providing a performance appraisal at the end of the person's first six months.

- What training objectives do you want the new team member to meet within their next six months?

During the induction process there should be the opportunity for the new team member to give you feedback. It is not a controlling activity from you as a manager. So here are a few ideas of questions you might ask the new hire. Give them the questions in advance of a meeting with you to give them time to prepare.

- Generally speaking, what do you think of your recruitment process?
- Which of our team's/organization's strong points struck you first?
- What was the first fault or weakness that became apparent to you?
- What reassured you?
- What worried you?
- Looking back, what useful information was not communicated to you when you were hired or started the job?
- If you were to employ someone into the company, what would you do in addition to what you yourself experienced?

Key tasks

- Think about organic growth of the team; could you promote someone from within your team, rather than hiring someone new?

- Review the techniques you use when interviewing staff in order to attract 'winners'. Do you 'sell' from the start the benefits of joining your organization?

- Treat candidates as your top priority by preparing for them as you would a customer! Use the recruitment process to showcase your organization's diverse teams, programmes, culture, business, employee networks, etc.

- Involve as many stakeholders as you can in the interview process.

- Make your induction programme fit for purpose. What needs to be developed or changed, or fine tuned? Give new hires total support through a robust induction process. Encourage feedback from them throughout to improve it next time.

05

Holistic Management

Introduction

If you analyse your operational role as a manager, it divides broadly into four parts – performance management, day-to-day operational work doing tasks that are repetitive, undertaking one-off or multiple projects, and running or attending meetings. We are exploring performance management throughout the rest of this book, and so this chapter will firstly focus on how you should best be using your time in working towards departmental and corporate objectives. Secondly, we will explore the people element of running projects – who you need to influence and how to do it, and thirdly running meetings so you achieve an agreed outcome.

The 80/20 rule – managing your time

To manage time well you have to believe in your own knowledge. If you know a weekly meeting takes thirty minutes, don't convince yourself that today it will only take fifteen minutes simply because you have more to do. If you have to be somewhere in ten minutes and you have ten minutes to get there, don't make one more phone call simply because you want to get it out of the way. People who manage their time badly seem to want to be unrealistic and go out of their way to create out-of-control situations. MARK MCCORMACK

Sometimes hard work and long hours aren't enough to keep you on top of your workload. Don't we all wish we had a 26 hour day? There never seems to be enough time to do everything. The reality is that in the current harsh economic climate we are all being asked to do more with less. You need to get your priorities right. This is one of the keys to good time management.

It might seems glaringly obviously, but we don't always do it: aim to do the important things first. Remember the Pareto principle, the 80/20 rule. This says 80 per cent of reward comes from 20 per cent of effort. One of the aims of time management is to refocus your mind to give more attention and time to the most important 20 per cent. The shift is on focus – concentrating on results, not on being busy.

Regrettably, habits are powerful. Ones that need changing may take some effort to shift, but once new ones are established, then they make the approaches they prompt at least semi-automatic. Getting to grips with managing your time effectively may well take a conscious effort, but by establishing good working habits the process gets easier as you go along.

The problem is we are all quite good at procrastinating. This could be, for example, because we are unsure how to tackle a particular assignment, dislike the task, or prefer another (despite the clear priority). Kate Muir in the *Sunday Times* (31 May 2008) wrote a heartfelt article about procrastination ('The Dark Ages'). Her premise was that she personally loved deadlines, as she is by nature an 'arousal procrastinator' – which, according to the online magazine *Slate,* is a person who 'seeks the excitement and pumping stress hormones of having to finish everything under duress'!

Well, if you don't fit into this category, as many of us don't, a little conscious effort and planning can make all the difference to our lives.

So as a starting point, here is a four-step process to help you become more organized and focused in your everyday activities.

Step 1 The planning process

- List all tasks and activities, and be aware of the time required to do them.

Step 2 Decide priorities

- There will be urgent tasks, when you have to react to situations. Some of these will also be important because they contribute towards your longer-term goals. (Category A)

- There will be proactive tasks that contribute towards the achievement of the job purpose. These may not be urgent, but they are important. (Category B)

- However, many of these reactive tasks, while being urgent, may also be relatively unimportant. They must be done, but not at the expense of the important tasks. (Category C)

- There will also be other tasks that are both relatively unimportant and of lower urgency. (Category D)

- There are some other things that should never be done at all.

So is the task urgent or important? The urgency of a task should suggest *when* it should be done. The importance of a task should suggest *how long* you should spend on it (see Figure 5.1).

Figure 5.1 Importance and urgency of task and activities

IMPORTANCE

Low	High		
Category C High urgency Low importance	**Category A** High importance High urgency	High	**URGENCY**
Category D Low importance Low urgency	**Category B** High importance Low urgency	Low	

Firstly, consider every item on the list of tasks or activities. Decide which category each task or activity falls into. Having done this you can now clearly see when things have to be done, and how much time should be allocated to each task.

Step 3 Delegate when appropriate

Having decided what needs to be done and the order or priority, the next question is 'Who should do it?'

In many cases the answer will be 'me' simply because there may not be anyone else who can do it. However many you have in your team, there still can be situations when you are the only person available. However, in many situations it may be possible to delegate work to members of the team (Figure 5.2).

Category A High importance – high urgency

- Do it yourself now – spend as long as it takes.

Category B High importance – low urgency

- Consider delegating parts to an experienced and proven member of the team.
- Schedule time for completion.

Figure 5.2 Delegation matrix

IMPORTANCE

Low	High		
Category C Delegate, have it done soon	**Category A** Do it now, yourself	High	**URGENCY**
Category D Delegate and keep an eye	**Category B** Delegate to experienced person	Low	

Category C High urgency – low importance

- Consider delegating as a development opportunity.
- Get it done soon.

Category D Low importance – low urgency

- Delegate, have it done sometime.
- Keep an eye on it.

There are going to be certain activities, such as meeting with colleagues, opening mail, responding to e-mails, that are not so time-critical but still need to be taken into account. So in planning your diary you need to put in the time-critical activities and deadlines, but also schedule in the non-time-critical tasks in the gaps.

So in brief:

Step 4 Plan your time

- Prepare a daily 'to do' list, ideally at the end of the previous day.
- Schedule time for Category A, high-priority, high-urgency tasks.
- Allow time for reactive tasks.
- Plan sufficient time for regular tasks that you know about (mentioned above).
- Schedule time each day for planning.
- Block out time and batch together reports to read, or performance reviews to approve, to maximize the use of the mental set-up time needed for the task.
- When is your prime time? It is not always first thing in the morning – it could be a little later in the day. We all have different 'creativity rhythms' – find out when yours is and plan accordingly.
- Set deadlines and give yourself 'rewards' when you meet them.
- Have a visible, high-impact reminder of your job purpose to keep you focused on what's important.
- Improve reading skills – scan faster.

Coming to terms with time wasters

- Manage your e-mails and phone calls – don't let them manage you. Check your mail first thing in the morning, early afternoon and just before you leave, unless you need an hourly update for some reason. It's too much of a temptation to react to mail messages rather than keeping focused on identified key activities.

- The more senior you are, the more selective you need to be about when you can take calls.

- If someone pops into your office, and you don't want to be disturbed, stand up and walk towards them – they won't think to stay.

- Recondition the expectation of others with regard to your availability and their claim on your time. Be realistic and pragmatic in this context, but remind people of the best time for you to talk or meet – 'can we discuss this further at our weekly meeting…', etc.

- Optionally, put your desk in a position that means your back is to the door – much less welcoming…!

- In turn, of course, be conscious of wasting other people's time.

- De-clutter the desk you work on. Don't have piles of unfinished proposals or partially finished projects immediately in your eye line. It can be distracting, and take you focus off what you are working on at the time.

- Start and finish one job at a time – avoid 'butterflying' between different assignments.

- When sifting through the mail each morning, if you can take action immediately with little effort involved – do that task. Then prioritize all other paperwork. Aim to only handle a piece of paper once.

Reviewing your working activities will almost certainly highlight the two key activities in your day:

- project-related activities;
- attending and running meetings.

So now we will move on to looking at these topics in more depth.

The people element of managing projects

Projects should be delivered on time, and on budget. It's often quoted that 52 per cent of all projects finish at 189 per cent of their initial budget. Many projects launch and are not completed.

The purpose of this chapter is not to analyse the use of practical project management tools but to focus instead on the behavioural and motivational elements that lead to any project being a success or not. While the nature of projects can be very diverse, the approach below applies in all cases.

Let's start by looking at a definition of a project. True projects share some common characteristics. They have to have clear and agreed objectives. Without them there is no sense of direction and no way to measure success. They have a defined lifespan, and generally involve working on something that is new or involves a one-time effort. They have three specific requirements (time, cost and performance are the basics).

What are project stakeholders looking for?

Besides obviously getting the project completed, too many project managers just focus on the process itself – setting up, planning, delivering and reviewing the outcome. This is not enough. Project managers that build a good reputation think of the project process from another viewpoint, that of their direct manager and also the end-users – in other words, the stakeholders. This means they are concerned with two different measures. Management wants a result in terms of value or cost, and end-users want a result that's best for them. Cost refers to a wide range of expenditures, but a narrow version, excluding general overheads, is simply the cost of the project team members. If the project team works effectively and easily then the cost per unit of project volume or value goes down, and management is happy. In other words they are considered efficient. It's obvious that if the project process is made 'easier' then project efficiency should rise. Conversely, if the project is made 'harder' efficiency will fall.

Raising efficiency of the project

There are many factors working to making running a project easier or harder, and most of these are under the project manager's control. Project teams have high project efficiency when:

- the project manager makes team working a pleasure;
- they make it easy for stakeholders to engage with the project team.

So much in a working environment is about word of mouth. If you are the project manager the aim is for you and your team to be seen as good to work with. You therefore have not only operational activities to do, but also a PR element to your work. You need to build and maintain strong personal relationships as well as getting the 'right' level of professional service throughout the project. You also need to be the communication channel both up and down, and be a good networker so that you can gain internal resources for the project, as you rarely work in isolation from the rest of the organization. In other words, you need to create a 'circle of influence'.

This ultimately means that if you deliver the project aims and meet stakeholder needs, they are likely to act as 'active references' for you and your team. So:

- they will 'self-refer' back to you when they need more;
- they will recommend the project team to others;
- they will quite often be willing to recommend the team to third parties.

Let's look at this relationship-building process in more detail, and see how you can get the project off to a good start.

Relationship building from the stakeholders' perspective

What are stakeholders fundamentally looking for?

1 Security – that you will deliver on time and within budget. Your active reference should endorse this.

2 Your having understood all parties' needs – both the sponsors' and the end-users'.

So how can you show you have understood their needs? By gathering in-depth information from both parties, listening and creating documentation as 'terms of reference'.

Gathering information from both parties

Asking the right questions

Firstly, you must understand end-users needs and motivations. It's great if you have 'terms of reference', but you will still need to ask questions to understand who will benefit, how they will benefit, how your project interfaces with other projects, etc.

Take the example of when you walk into a garden centre and say 'I want to buy a spade.' That is certainly a clear statement, but the information is insufficient. To ensure you get the right spade the salesperson should know:

- who is going to use it (a professional gardener can handle a bigger, heavier implement than an unfit amateur; tall users need longer shafts);
- what for (a big blade for digging over large, clear areas, a small one for work amongst the shrubbery);
- what sort of soil (stony or heavy clay soils suggest a strong narrow blade, lighter soil a wide one);
- what budget is available.

Only with this information can the salesperson really help. Project managers, too, should know a lot about their subject and understand how the various project products/services match different user requirements. Rational recommendations only come if you really probe and find out all the relevant information.

Actively listen

This is a difficult art, since you have to hear what they say, convert it to a mental picture or actual diagram, make notes, etc all the while listening to the next sentence. Check for understanding throughout, and reconfirm the information that you have collected at the end of the brief.

Defining terms of reference

Your 'terms of reference' are akin to a sales proposal. Project terms of reference, besides containing an overview of the project, clarify the issues to be addressed by the project.

Construct your terms of reference by including:

- information about the business problem (the needs the project is to address);

- information about the end-user's or stakeholder's 'desires' and 'wants';

- concrete knowledge of their current situation and the future 'desired' situation;

- any special terms and conditions that must be considered during the project cycle;

- the purpose of the project, and timed deliverables.

The terms of reference are often distributed to quite a large audience. Check with a colleague beforehand to ensure that the document contains the right 'tone' to appeal to the final audience, and to pick up on any special omissions or unclear points. A technical audience will expect quite a lot of technical depth. A non-technical and senior management audience may just want an overview of the technical aspects and will be more interested in (and persuaded) by a business benefit oriented wording. This should concentrate on how the project helps them to overcome problems and meet their needs or become more effective.

Pascal, the famous French philosopher, said 'We are more convinced by the reasons which we have found ourselves than by those given by others.' For project sponsors to sign off on the project they must say 'yes' to each step of the terms of reference. They will readily do this if they recognize their own words in the document, ie their own evidence and reasons needed for this project.

Projects will inevitably take a substantial part of your working time. Attending or running meetings will also take time, so it is important to ensure that you are attending appropriate sessions, and if you run a meeting, that you make the best use of the time.

Tips and techniques

Questions to ask yourself whilst running a project

- Do you really understand the business issues? Do the terms of reference reflect these?

- Have you steered the decision maker, facilitated his or her clarification of the issues to create a vision/way forward, *prior* to coming up with the solution yourself?

- Who are the real decision makers? Who has got the power? Are you engaging with them sufficiently?

- Are you measuring success criteria? Remember that you as an owner are looking for value for money. The end-user is looking for a solution.

- Make sure at the evaluation stage that the project has delivered the change as indicated in the terms of reference.

Getting meetings to work effectively

A meeting is an expensive use of an organization's most valuable resource: the time of its staff. They not only take time, but have an underlying cost. There are the direct costs of bringing people together and holding the meeting itself, but also the lost time for those involved not doing their normal work. Having said this, properly run meetings can ultimately save time, increase productivity, produce new ideas, and get real 'buy in' from stakeholders. There is nothing like a face-to-face experience for being effective. Videoconferencing can, of course, be effective, particularly with virtual teams, but this only works well with top specification systems that emulate participants sitting around a table.

There are a variety of meetings held in organizations. Some are purely to pass on information. Others might be for legal reasons – such as board and annual general meetings. In this section we are going to explore action and objectives meetings (or review meetings), where assessments are made of projects or people, and actions decided. The principles we will be exploring will also apply to those that are held for creative purposes, to find new solutions or improve existing ones. Quality circles, brainstorming sessions and freewheeling are all examples of these types of meetings.

Stage 1 Preparation

Meetings *must* have concrete/SMART objectives – usually agreeing actions or changes – and these should either be achieved, or conclusions drawn as to why not and what has to be done next.

People need to be carefully and appropriately selected, and be clear about why they have been invited, what they are expected to contribute, and what decisions are to be taken.

The agenda should be very narrowly defined, so that everyone invited can contribute to each item. However, sometimes a great deal of expense is involved in gathering the participants together, so a wide-ranging agenda may be necessary. Most project-oriented meetings have a typical agenda boiling down to:

- Where are we compared with the plan, time and budget (have any items joined or left the critical path?)?

- What unexpected successes have we achieved?

- What unexpected problems have turned up and what shall we do about them?

- What are the plans for the next period?

Decide what the outcome for each issue is, and put this on the agenda alongside the item heading.

In your agenda it is important to put a guideline timing against each topic to keep the meeting on track. Allow for plenty of short five-minute breaks if the meeting is to be long. People can only concentrate for about 45 minutes. Ensure the timing of the meeting causes the least disruption to all concerned. Start and finish times should be indicated on the agenda.

Stage two of preparation

Let's look at a few simple 'mechanical' aspects of preparation.

The invitation should contain the names of all those invited, the venue (with a map and details of public transport or parking facilities as relevant), the date, start and end times, and the agenda with overall objectives and item-specific objectives. Anyone expected to make a presentation should be identified and all participants should be formally instructed to make relevant preparations.

Make sure that all formal presentations are circulated to participants long enough beforehand for them to have an opportunity to digest the information. This element of preparation saves enormous amounts of meeting time.

Agenda items should be listed in order of priority. As we have mentioned above in the time management section, work out a prioritizing process along the lines of urgent/not urgent and important/not important. Get the urgent and important matters at the top of the agenda since participants will still be fresh (and it will encourage punctuality). If individuals are not needed for all items then juggle the list so that they can arrive late or leave early, rather than rushing in and out.

Don't have an 'Any other business' (AOB) item. The objectives of the meeting are clearly set out, and if someone has something to contribute that is relevant to an agenda item that is when they should speak. AOB gives people an opportunity to waffle, waste time and ride their irrelevant personal hobby horses. If someone wants to raise an additional topic relevant to either the main subject matter or the people at the meeting, have it added to the agenda and so dealt with properly.

Obvious other preparatory measures: book the room and make sure it stays booked (and that there are enough chairs). Organize coffee/tea/lunch as appropriate. Assign someone outside the meeting room to take messages on behalf of those attending. Make sure any visual aids are present and working. If relevant, assign a minute note-taker.

The meeting itself

An effective meeting is crisp, clear and as brief as is possible while reaching concrete objectives. The onus is on the chairperson to make this happen. This could be you or a colleague. A poorly chaired meeting tends to ramble, to wander off-track to explore byways and to waste time.

If you are chairing the meeting it is therefore essential to set the correct 'tone' right from the start. This means starting at the pre-advised time of commencement, not 10 or 15 minutes later waiting for stragglers to come in. Bang on time. You should be able to define the purpose of the meeting in one or two sentences and summarize the objectives.

Ask participants if they are prepared to commit to the agenda.

Establish a few ground rules, for example the confidentiality of the information discussed (if relevant) and the need for everyone to participate and to reach closure on each topic.

Keep the objectives in mind and 'Go for the close' on each topic as quickly as possible. Some people make little prompt cards for each item, with two or three phrases to represent the main decisions to be taken or questions answered and use them to keep discussions on track.

Make sure everyone understands and agrees with (or has been overruled but accepts) the conclusions and that they are recorded accurately on a 'protocol' sheet before moving to the next topic. This sheet should include what actions are to be taken, by whom and by when. Get the collected protocols photocopied and distributed before the meeting breaks up.

The agenda should ideally have a time limit for each subject; if you make up time this will allow a little latitude for particularly contentious items, or, better still, you can all go back to work (or home) a few minutes earlier. Finish by the appointed time, even if this means dropping the lowest priority agenda items.

Sometimes there is a threat of overrun because it became evident during the meeting that an additional topic really needs to be considered. Ideally, put it on the agenda for the next meeting or convene a special meeting restricted to just the relevant people. At worst adjourn the present meeting for 20 minutes to allow some preparation time and then restart. However, the primary purpose of distributing working papers ahead of the meeting is to ensure that this sort of problem doesn't arise, since the need for extra discussion should have been foreseen.

In keeping with this air of efficiency and onwards momentum, do not tolerate:

- digressions – no one will be prepared so they just waste time;
- chatter by people not fully engaged in the subject matter under discussion. If they don't stop talking, as chairperson stop the meeting, leave a pause, and then say you cannot continue the meeting until everyone is fully focused;
- mobile telephones in the meeting room – if people are expecting calls have them give contact details of the appointed message-taker, who can relay the information at the next break.

After the meeting

Get the minutes written up while they are still fresh in your mind. The protocols recording specific actions should be appended, and everything distributed within one or two days to participants, to those who were unable to attend and, possibly section by section, to others with specific interests in individual items. The meeting should have induced some momentum into work on the subjects discussed. Receiving the minutes within 24 hours sends a positive message and reinforces that momentum. A delay can have a converse effect.

If the meeting has involved extra work in preparation for some individuals, or particularly onerous travel, write a short note to these people to thank them for their time and trouble: it boosts morale and does your personal 'image' no harm.

If you called the meeting, then the work described in the protocols is presumably necessary to enable you to meet your own objectives. So follow up. Mark in your diary the deadline dates, and reminders to yourself to check progress a few days before the deadlines (or earlier/more often as the case dictates).

Key tasks

- Are you using your time effectively? Make a deliberate effort to monitor how you spend your time using a time log, and use the *delegation matrix* as a prompt to get the correct balance of your work.
- Make a conscious effort during projects to get others on your side to act as an 'active reference'. Remember that project management is more than an operational activity.
- When you next run a meeting, make sure people attending understand why they have been invited, what they are expected to contribute, and what decisions are to be taken. Keep the meeting on track, don't have AOB on the agenda, and create a protocol sheet of ongoing actions required and time frames to be adhered to. Always monitor actions agreed to ensure they are completed to your satisfaction.

06

The power of motivation

Introduction

As you grow your business and take on staff you are going to need to know how to motivate others.

Motivation is a powerful tool. In the hand of you as a manager it can persuade, convince and propel individuals or teams to take action. There's one caveat, however: you have to be motivated yourself in order to motivate others to work optimally. The concept of motivation – think of 'employee engagement' – is generally viewed in terms of staff feeling a strong emotional bond to the organization, demonstrating a willingness to recommend the organization to others, and committing time and effort to helping the organization succeed.

In business, average performance is carried out at 70 per cent of the available knowledge and energy of each member of staff. This means that there is a 'secret' reserve of no less than 30 per cent you as a manager can utilize. If this is true, and there is no reason to doubt it, it should be a challenge for every manager as to how you can mobilize this 30 per cent. Motivation is a basic aspect in every work situation. Managers fail, simply because they do not understand those whom they relate to or they are taken up by their desire to satisfy their own needs, so that the needs of those whom they cooperate with are not a priority or simply forgotten.

Defining motivation

The *Shorter Oxford English Dictionary* defines 'motivation' as causing someone to act in a particular way. So by your words and actions you can 'cause people to act' positively and productively, or negatively and destructively. It is commonplace that a highly motivated group of average players runs rings round a team of demotivated star players. Psychologists have devised experiments to quantify the difference. In slightly exaggerated form, this may be summarized as 'two for the price of one' or 'one motivated person is worth two who are not'. Productivity and quality can differ by up to a factor of two, depending on the motivation of the people involved. The impact of this difference on competitiveness is hard to overstate. High levels of motivation maintained consistently over the long term can easily make the difference between failure and success, growth and stagnation, becoming a recognized 'winner' and disappearing.

Motivation requisites:

- Managers have to be motivated to motivate.
- Motivation requires a goal.
- Motivation, once established, does not last if not repeated.
- Motivation requires recognition.
- Participation has motivating effects.
- Seeing oneself making progress motivates individuals.
- Challenges only motivate if individuals feel they can win.
- Everybody has a motivational fuse, ie everybody can be motivated.
- Belonging to a group motivates.

What is motivation?

Motivation is inspiring others to work, individually or in groups. For managers, the goal of motivation is that it delivers discretionary effort. This means getting team members to go the extra mile when undertaking a task or assignment. Motivation requires a goal. It is about taking action. Motivation applies to the entire class of drives, desires, needs, wishes and similar forces. It is getting somebody to do something because they want to do it. Since all of us are motivated by differing forces, when we say that managers motivate we mean that they do those things that they hope will satisfy these drives and desires and induce their reports to act in a desired manner. Motivation is the willingness to take efforts towards realizing goals, conditioned by the efforts and ability to satisfy individual needs. Motivating others means understanding:

- what is important to them – their *values*;
- what they want to do with their life – their *goals*;
- what *beliefs* will help them get what they want;
- what *skills* will help them to realize their dreams.

The process of motivation

Motivation requires individuals to be aware of a need or desire. This energizes them and gets their attention in satisfying this need.

Figure 6.1 Step-by-step motivation process

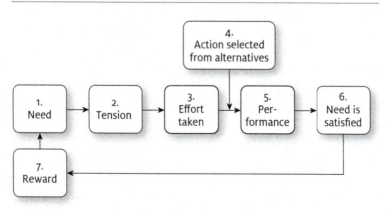

What 'needs' motivate people?

One of the most widely mentioned theories of motivation is Maslow's hierarchy of needs. Maslow sought to explain *why people are driven by particular needs at particular times*. Why does one person spend considerable time and energy on personal safety and another on pursuing the esteem of others? Maslow saw human needs in the form of a hierarchy, ascending from the lowest to the highest, ie from the most pressing to the least pressing.

Maslow's hierarchy of needs is shown in Figure 6.2. In their order of importance, they are physiological, safety, social, esteem, and self-actualization needs. A person will try to satisfy the most important needs first. When a person succeeds in satisfying this, it will cease being a current motivator, and the person will try to satisfy the next most important need.

For example, a starving man (priority 1) will not take an interest in the latest happenings in the art world (priority 5), nor in how he is viewed or esteemed by others (priority 3 or 4), nor even whether he feels secure (priority 2).

Maslow supposes that even the essentially satisfied person has room for growth. He believes our need for self-realization and performance is never completely satisfied. One success inspires us to take on the next thing... and the next. In this way we achieve a 'feeling of well-being' that is too agreeable to give up. On the other hand, we must be careful that our failures, or our fear of failure, doesn't make us give up before we start. We all know those who will tell you why something won't work before they have even tried it.

What are sample needs that get people 'moving' to satisfy something? They are about HAVING, DOING and BEING, as shown in the table.

In the 1960s Herzberg proposed that a person's needs break down into two categories, hygiene factors and motivator factors – in other words, 'what makes you work? ' and 'what makes you work well?' He used the term 'job enrichment' to describe how the motivator factors can be used to achieve higher levels of satisfaction with a job.

Figure 6.2　Maslow's needs applied to Herzberg's motivation–hygiene theory

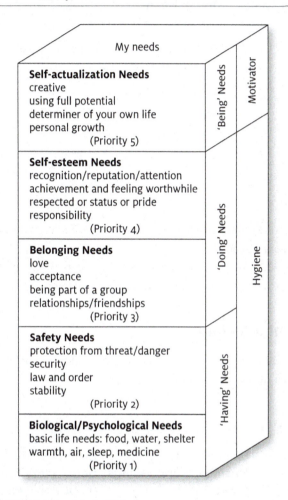

SOURCE After Hopson and Scally 1984

This job enrichment is now very familiar to us in the twenty-first century. Herzberg suggested you could enrich a job by giving a person a complete natural unit of work, having a periodical reporting system rather than tight inspection and control, and giving a person responsibility and also accountability. He also suggested giving a specific task to enable them to become expert in that field,

Table 6.1   Sample needs that motivate people

'Having' Needs	'Doing' Needs	'Being' Needs
security	work with others	learning
money	community	independence
routine	friendship	creativity
peace	contact with people	challenge
	recognition	help society
	being expert	risk
	promotion	status

SOURCE Hopson and Scally 1984

plus periodically introducing new and more difficult tasks for self-development purposes.

Figure 6.2 sums up Maslow's levels of needs when applied to Herzberg's motivation–hygiene theory described above.

Needs and feelings

Let's look at examples of how feeling can impact on our ability to act in each of the hierarchical levels (Table 6.2).

Table 6.2   How feelings can impact on our ability to act

NEEDS	Examples of Unsatisfactory Feelings (to be Avoided)	Examples of Satisfactory Feelings (to be Achieved)
Priority 5 Self-actualization	boredom, egoism, futility, keeping away, inhibition, inflexibility, dependence, immaturity, imperfection	creativity, growth, maturity, openness, independence, curiosity, determination, sensitivity, flexibility, spontaneity, altruism, sense of reality

(continued)

Table 6.2   *(Continued)*

NEEDS	Examples of Unsatisfactory Feelings (to be Avoided)	Examples of Satisfactory Feelings (to be Achieved)
Priority 4 Self-esteem needs	failure, defeat, disgrace, unsuitability, humiliation, contempt, guilt, unimportance, ignorance, ignobility, being the scapegoat	pride, success, prestige, honour, victory, esteem, self-confidence, respect, skill, recognition, praise, talent, heroism
Priority 3 Belonging (social) needs	rejection, loneliness, neglect, exclusion, isolation, criticism, incomprehension, disapproval, embarrassment, reprimand	acceptance, solidarity, support, relationship, understanding, popularity, friendship, attention, compliment, involvement
Priority 2 Safety needs	doubt, worry, danger, loss, confusion, insecurity, fear, chaos, concern, sorrow, internal conflict, threat	security, safety, reassurance, confidentiality, peace of mind, tranquility, harmony, certainty, stability, order
Priority 1 Biological/ physiological needs	hunger, thirst, drowsiness, fever, sickness, discomfort, weakness, heat, cold, uneasiness, fatigue	fullness, saturation, leisure, watchfulness, health, warmth, strength, pleasantness, enjoyment, rest, relaxation, excitement

When a member of your team says '*I want*' this is related to one of their needs. In order to really understand and really relate to others, managers must learn to speak in terms of their (underlying) needs, instead of relying on what someone actually says they want.

Motivators

How can managers motivate team members? Let's look at:

discretionary effort motivation;

intrinsic motivation;

extrinsic motivation.

Discretionary effort motivation, also known as 'discretionary energy', is the effort or 'energy' employees choose to exert (or not) at work. Employers hire people to perform. Their willingness to perform above and beyond basic job requirements is a reflection of their willingness to engage discretionary effort. This willingness is influenced by the quality of a manager's interactions. The more discretionary effort managers tap into, the better.

Intrinsic motivators are when individuals are motivated by intrinsic factors (eg personal growth or development, working to a common purpose, values, being part of a larger purpose). Intrinsic motivation comes about by the work we do, and from the pleasure a person gets from simply working on a task, or the sense of satisfaction in completing it. Intrinsic refers to our understanding of our responsibilities, and knowledge of our freedom to act, etc.

Intrinsically motivated team members work on a task because it is enjoyable, and they love to work on finding a solution to a problem because the challenge of finding a solution provides pleasure. This form of motivation does not mean, however, that a person will not seek rewards. It just means that such external rewards are not enough to keep a person motivated. The more attuned team members are to intrinsic motivators, the more receptive they are likely to be to organizational values. However, this can be undermined if they perceive things are not fair (eg pay) or there is a lack of even-handedness and professionalism in the way managers behave.

Extrinsic motivation relates to organizational rewards or any motivation that comes from outside an individual. Such rewards provide satisfaction and pleasure that the task itself may not provide. Extrinsic motivation does not mean, however, that a person will not get any pleasure from working on or completing a task. It just means that the pleasure they anticipate from some external reward will continue to be a motivator even when the task to be done holds little or no interest. The rewards can be as minor as a smiling face or a bonus.

What are other motivators managers can draw on?

Affiliation motivation: This is a drive team members have to relate to others on a social basis. Persons with affiliation motivation perform work better when they are complimented for their favourable attitudes and cooperation.

Competence motivation: This is the drive team members have to be good at something, allowing them to perform high-quality work. Competence motivated people seek job mastery. Besides achievement, they take pride in developing and using their competence. They strive to be creative when confronted with obstacles. They learn from their experience.

Power motivation: This is the drive team members have to influence people and change situations. Power-motivated people wish to create an impact on their organization and are willing to take risks to do so.

Attitude motivation: Attitude motivation is how team members think and feel about the future and how they react to the past and obstacles that come their way. They have self-confidence and a belief in themselves. Their positive attitude to life and their ability to handle situations is paramount. These people will never tell you why something won't work before they have even tried it.

Incentive motivation: This is where a team member or a team reaps a reward from an activity. It is 'you do this and you get that' attitude. It is the types of awards and prizes that drive people to work harder.

Fear motivation: Fear motivation coerces team members to act against their will. This applies in difficult economic periods where managers can threaten to close down part of a business unit, re-categorize job titles or demote personnel. It can be helpful in the short run in that it gets the job done quickly. (NB! Individual team members can be motivated by the fear of failure.)

Expectancy motivation (Vroom's expectancy theory): The processes team members undergo when making choices. It is a motivation theory that predicts team members are motivated when they believe that:

- putting in more effort will yield better job performance;
- better job performance will lead to organizational rewards, such as an increase in salary or benefits;
- predicted organizational rewards are valued by the team member in question.

This theory suggests that managers should align rewards, expected behaviours and goals directly to performance and that rewards are deserved and wanted by team members. Team members' self-interest in wanting the rewards is key. Behaviour results from conscious choices among variables whose purpose it is to maximize pleasure and to minimize pain. The product of these variables is the motivation.

So, fine, we have explored a range of options you might use for motivation purposes. Let's see this in action.

Motivation application

Consider an individual. Let's call him Peter. He is doing a good job and says he wants to go on a training course. So what is he really seeking? What need or needs is he trying to satisfy?

If Peter wants to attend training, he may describe his motive as wanting to further his career. At a deeper level, he may be trying to impress others. At a still deeper level, he may want to attend the courses because it helps him feel smart and up-to-date. When Peter looks at a particular course, he will react not only to its stated learning objectives but also to those other cues, not necessarily being aware of that himself.

Peter's manager doesn't really want Peter to go on this course. He doesn't really need a better-skilled team member. He does need, however, to be aware of the possibility of Peter's deeper motives and decide to either send him on the course or come up with other means of satisfying Peter's (subconscious) needs. But one way or another something will have to be done or Peter's 30 per cent reserve may not be utilized.

What light does Maslow's theory throw on Peter's interest in attending training?

We can guess that Peter has satisfied his physiological (he looks healthy), safety (he earns enough to pay the bills, his performance gives him good job security), and social needs (he is happily married and has several good friends); so these are not the needs that motivate him.

His interest might come from a strong need for more esteem from others or from a higher need for self-actualization. He wants to actualize his potential as an intelligent person through learning to master the latest skills and to give himself every chance of career promotion.

What are the threats for the manager? Peter might get frustrated at not being able to put what he has learned into practice. Senior managers and colleagues might see Peter as a threat. A lot of that can be prevented by good communication all round. Peter's manager should talk with him and explain his thinking (with reasons why) for sending him/not sending him on the course. Peter's manager should also talk with senior management to explain the benefits of Peter attending the course and the positive impact on them and the team/organization. The manager's role is to explain his or her decisions to all concerned, and while others might feel threatened or upset at least they know the context of the manager's decision.

Motivation in practice

We have looked at some processes from which motivation arises. What are sample things you, as a manager, can do to improve your capacity to motivate team members?

- **Understand what the needs of your team members are,** expressed by Maslow: security, social acceptance, appreciation and self-realization. Not only finding out what their needs are, but also what they want. You may not be able to satisfy their wishes, but you can at least try to modify your approach to motivation in the light of these facts. Find out by asking your team members using open questions.

- **Money** is not the only reward that people need and want. It is a hygiene factor and not always a motivator, and even if it is, it may last only a short time. People are motivated by acknowledgement, appreciation, promotion, the work itself and by the opportunity to achieve something extra or by having more responsibilities. The latter rewards may be more effective than money. It depends on the individual needs. Understanding these needs will enable you to give rewards more effectively.

- A reward will be much more effective if team members know what they will receive if they do a good and efficient job. It's therefore necessary that:

  - you point out what the relation between the performances accomplished and the financial reward;

  - you indicate to your team members the concrete objectives they must meet. Of course, these must be demanding *and* attainable;

  - they are aware that their performance will be acknowledged and appreciated, financially rewarded or will lead to a job with more responsibilities. Do not make attaining these rewards too easy. Express appreciation for results and efforts;

  - you explain what team members must do to be eligible for promotion, or to attain more responsibilities;

- you make it clear what the result will be for the organization and themselves, when they perform badly.

- Be aware that the objective of motivation, as defined by Douglas McGregor (1960), consists of *creating the conditions* by which the team members can achieve their own targets best. McGregor summarized the different views of employee perception by management, which had been expressed in his time, into 'Theory X' and 'Theory Y'. The theory says that managers need to treat their staff as fully adult, independent, responsible and valued human beings who are no different to themselves, but with different needs. It is by recognizing those needs and acting upon them appropriately that team members can be fully engaged so as to perform to their full potential:

  - determining the factors that annoy team members and *openly committing yourself* to eliminating them;

  - determining the needs of the team members, so that you try to *match the rewards* to the needs;

  - using a scheme that *makes team members decide themselves what they can do* and should do, and determine aligned team targets and standards that must be met.

- Acknowledge that team members can be *satisfied by the work itself*, if their work satisfies the need of responsibility and achievement. Do this by using the following motivating methods:

  increase team member responsibilities;

  - give then more room to vary their working methods, the order and the pace;

  - do not use too much supervision – make very clear to team members that they are themselves responsible for the targets and standards to be achieved;

  - give team members the information necessary for checking whether their work conforms to the requirements and how you plan to monitor their performance;

  - encourage the participation of team members in drawing up new action plans and in applying innovative methods.

Consider doing the following exercise with team members.

Exercise

Action 1 Seven types of motivation

You can improve your team members' motivation by completing a list of current and to-be-achieved objectives or goals (for each team member) listed under the seven types of motivation above. Involve your team members in doing these. The purpose is to check if you have a good balance of motivators. Regularly ask your team members to update this list, since, once needs get fulfilled, others will arise. Don't forget to prioritize the motivational factors not yet achieved.

Action 2 Playing Herzberg

First of all list all the hygiene factors or elements you think should be present in order to obtain a normal working environment. Indicate whether these elements are actually present or not. It's important is that you make up this list on your own but based on the knowledge you have of your team members and on what they find lacking in the department. Communicate with them!

Allow yourself at least one month to complete the list with items you gather from conversations with your team members. Obviously, the elements they indicate will usually be hygiene factors that are lacking. Be careful to distinguish clearly between the hygiene factors and the motivating factors.

Action 3 Playing Maslow

Complete a list of how much you know about your team members. Then analyse each team member in terms of where they are in Maslow's needs hierarchy to find more about their consequent levels of motivation.

You should also list their needs as they express them and their needs as seen through Maslow's eyes.

Action 4 Planning the motivation process

Together with the missing hygiene factors, list the most important needs for each team member separately. Each list helps you to visualize the current level of expectation of each team member. This will help you understand him or her better.

Some needs may be in the process of being satisfied, eg some persons are involved in a team-related project they enjoy. Such elements will help tilt the balance to the positive side. Verify the personal needs of each team member through 1:1 meetings with them. At the same time you will agree with them on ways of satisfying identified needs aligned with organizational objectives.

Finally, draw up a plan (keep thinking about team members involvement) in which your first goal is to eliminate missing hygiene factors. It's quite possible that you can increase your team member's potential to realize more organizational objectives if it is found that your team's potential is higher than assumed.

Key tasks

- Use Maslow's theory to understand the needs of your team members ie discover what motivates each of them.
- Do your team members know what reward they will receive if they do a good and efficient job?
- What satisfactory and unsatisfactory feelings are impacting your team's performance today?
- Carry out the four actions above to understand what you should do to improve motivation in your team.

07

Performance management

Introduction

Performance management is helping a member of your staff understand their role and responsibilities, and their individual contribution to realizing business objectives through achieving planned and agreed results. Many organizations also use performance management in career planning and personal development.

What does a member of staff expect from their manager?

- Where the team and individuals are headed. This is the business vision.

- Why they are headed there (and not somewhere else). This is the business mission or why the organization exists.

- What it looks like when they get there. How our objectives and efforts help us to deliver the organization's mission and business plans.

- How we should behave and work together as a team. This is all about the organization's culture.

So if you are recruiting someone into your team, jointly agree with them what you expect (and do not expect from them) in terms of performance and behaviours. This is where key results areas (KRA) and targets are required.

Key results areas flow from individual or team job descriptions. KRAs contribute towards clarifying *how we should (as a team) be spending our time*. For the team's strategy to succeed all team members must achieve specific results, which when accumulated, ensure that all strategy elements are delivered. KRAs are a summary of those key factors of an individual's job or the team's job that are vital for the team's success. They must be monitored, at a minimum, each month to ensure keeping on track with your strategy.

If you have difficulty identifying your KRAs ask yourself the following question: 'What are the major aspects of the team's work that could go wrong?' You might say 'We don't realize our sales target', 'We use up our resources', 'Too many customers complain' or 'We don't complete our reports on time'. These can be translated into the following KRAs – sales, finance, customer service and monthly reports.

Targets and objectives are the same thing; however, some organizations refer to strategic business and departmental objectives (these are longer term) and individual targets (these are short term), and agree them during annual performance reviews and regular team meetings.

Your role as a manager is to ensure performance bears a straight line relationship to what your organization is setting out to achieve. It's about planning, target setting, monitoring and reviewing.

Managing performance should focus on the achievement of business and team strategies by ensuring team members adopt the right competencies (behaviours) as well as delivering their objectives.

It's all about alignment. Alignment of people and processes, with clear organizational goals. What does this mean? Too often we see people and strategies/systems that unintentionally are misaligned with desired outcomes. Consequently, no matter how much harder or faster or longer people work, they are unable to achieve intended business results. If there's poor alignment with the organization's vision to guide staff, even the best intentioned cannot tell if they are headed in the right direction.

Think of a fabulous stained-glass window. The job of assembling all the pieces is much easier when we have a clear template to guide our efforts. When every piece of glass is placed in its proper position, everything makes sense. However, if pieces are put in upside down or sideways, the result cannot possibly be what was intended by the artist. Similarly, an organization whose people, strategies, and/or processes are misaligned with its vision cannot achieve its intended business outcomes.

Consider using 360° feedback to check alignment and behaviours. It's a fantastic tool since it provides honest feedback from subordinates, peers and managers (and, in some cases, feedback from external sources such as customers and suppliers or other interested stakeholders) rated against personal self-assessment. This type of feedback is contrasted with 'downward feedback', where team members are given feedback by their manager during a performance appraisal; 360° is more believable and may have a bigger impact than traditional manager–team member feedback, since it provides multiple perspectives that cannot be ignored.

Your management role and performance

A good manager will:

1 Clearly explain the team's objectives and put these in the context of the overall objectives of the organization and its *mission*.

- Be *accountable* for their actions whilst sharing the credit for team achievements with the whole team and being generous with praise and encouragement where this is due.

- Distribute *responsibilities and opportunities* suitably among the members of the team, taking account both of differing skills and abilities and of the need to encourage individual development.

- Encourage *individual development* but be realistic when discussing possibilities for further advancement and refrain from raising unwarranted expectations.

- Treat all staff, both within and outside the team, with due *respect* and insist that team members do the same.

- Ensure that there is frequent and open *communication* with their team members, which is fundamental to maintaining a high motivation and morale.

- Encourage team members to express their views and suggestions on the work and the working environment, and *listen* to what they have to say.

- Provide regular *feedback* on performance to individual team members.

- Address weaknesses as they arise, provide *coaching and assistance* as necessary, and deal fairly, but forthrightly, with those who prove unable to meet the required standards.

Reviewing and evaluating performance

As mentioned above, an essential part of your role as a manager is to be able to communicate effectively, motivate, boost morale and develop others. Reviewing and evaluating the performance of staff, and helping each individual to expand their skill sets and competencies will ultimately improve organizational performance and feed into business planning. Giving feedback should be part of your everyday activities, with the key milestone of a formal appraisal, usually undertaken on a half-yearly or an annual basis, to review a team member's performance, establish specific goals and objectives and discuss career interests and development needs and requirements.

Why bother? Because one-man teams don't work. Your job is to coordinate your team's effort to achieve organizational objectives. This is a tough job. Increasing productivity and adding value/profitability to organizations constantly having to reinvent themselves, owing to the pace of change, doesn't come easy. People get stressed, distracted, confused. Some jockey for position, some give up. They look at *you* to 'fix things', and even those who are willing to help can't agree on *how* things should be fixed. This is your challenge.

Balancing tasks and people

People in your team need to understand not only the task you have allocated to them, but also how it fits into the bigger activities going on in the team. Life as a manager is a constant balancing act, getting the right emphasis between task and people management. An imbalance between the two will affect team spirit and cooperation, and could, for example, spoil the chances for success during a project.

Too much *task* focus can show up as:

- pushing for results too soon;
- too much concern for efficiency and time;
- one or a few members plan experiments outside of team meetings;
- assignments handed out to team members outside of meetings.

This could result in:

- concerns being ignored;
- limited participation of some members;
- meetings discussion dominated by a few people;
- decisions that are made based on opinion, rather than based on facts provided by subject matter/technical support.

Too much *people* focus can show up as:

- too much concern for feelings and personal problems;
- letting discussions wander until everyone airs all their fears;
- trying to do everything by consensus decision making.

This could result in:

- project progress suffering;
- no forward progress;
- no milestones met;
- action items repeated or continually extended.

Giving effective feedback

Ken Blanchard's attitude to feedback is that it is the 'Breakfast of champions'. He believes great performers use feedback to enhance their performance. This may be so, but so often feedback can be misinterpreted and viewed in a negative light. The purpose of feedback is either to maintain or change performance, in order to keep an individual or team on track to achieve their work goals. Feedback should be viewed as a way of giving help. So you need to be sensitive, informative, and give ample time for the person you are reviewing to ask questions, and put forward their point of view.

There are different types of feedback that should be used according to the situation:

- *Motivational feedback* tells a person that their good performance has been noticed and recognized, and gives them the impetus to repeat this type of performance in the future. Feedback should be given as soon as possible after the event / activity has taken place. Be careful in this situation of giving extra advice or suggestions for even better performance at the same time, as this could be interpreted as criticism.

- *Development feedback* indicates to a person what needs to be improved, and asks them, for example, how they believe they could have tackled a task / situation in a different way in order to learn for the future. If you have to correct someone's performance do not do it in front of the rest of the team; whenever possible do it in private.

Correcting small issues like the layout of a proposal, or modification of a task, is usually quite straightforward. Needing to review and correct a person's behaviour can be more challenging, and we will look at this in more detail in Chapter 10 (Handling a problem with a team member).

Tips and techniques	**Giving effective feedback**

- Giving feedback should be about a person's performance or behaviour, not them as a person.
- Focus on facts and be objective.
- Keep calm even if the other person loses their temper.
- Make the exchange question-based if possible.
- Actively listen to the response, and re-clarify your understanding of the situation.
- Use the 'positive sandwich' approach – giving positive information first, followed by the negative information, and then finish on a positive note.

How you pass on information or communicate information will depend on the nature of work that you do. It's easier for a manager to give (negative) feedback than for a member of the team to do so. If you want to give (negative) feedback choose your time and place carefully! A neutral venue – not *their* office – and during an appraisal session or 1:1 meeting is usually best.

The annual performance and development review scheme

The annual performance and development review scheme is often described as 'the dreaded annual appraisal'. Why is this so? Because so often the process turns into an opportunity for the manager to focus on negative performance issues in the past year, rather than using the review session as a positive platform for creating plans for the future. Should a person be underperforming, this should have been discussed during informal meetings held between both parties throughout the year.

You have to bear in mind that this formal review process is an exacting situation for both parties. For the person being reviewed, if the appraisal is not objective, clear and fair, it can ultimately have an impact on promotion opportunities and send a career off track. For the person undertaking the appraisal review it can lead to legal headaches down the line if a person's performance is so poor that their job could be terminated. In turn a company can suffer if good performance is not acknowledged and rewarded appropriately, or poor performance is not highlighted and dealt with. Each organization has a different way of conducting annual or half-yearly appraisals, so see what is best for you. There could be a web-based template that you ask a member of staff to complete – or get your managers to write a report for you – annually about the performance of their team members. Or you could use a 360° degree annual appraisal process. One way or the other you need to be clear as to what you are expected to produce for review purposes.

The purpose of the appraisal process is to act as a catalyst to making future performance better than or simply different to that of the past. In this context it should:

- review the last year's performance of the person being reviewed;
- specifically identify what has gone well, and where there is room for improvement;
- plan future work, and the development of their role;
- clarify, define and redefine priories and objectives;
- agree specific goals;
- establish performance standards and expectations;
- set up a system that measures actual performance;
- identify where training and development might be needed;
- create a 'whole person' development plan;
- act as a catalyst for delegation;
- reinforce and cascade the organization's philosophy, values, aims, strategies and priorities.

Preparing for an appraisal

Many organizations have a prescriptive approach, and use a template appraisal form. Good documentation can act as a prompt but should not get in the way of open, honest discussion between both parties.

The appraisal form documentation should have been passed to the appraisee well in advance of the meeting. If you have not appraised the person in question before, you should jointly determine with them the key result areas (KRAs) of their role right from the start of their employment. KRAs are the person's primary responsibilities (or core accountabilities). KRAs capture about 80 per cent of the person's work role. The remainder is usually devoted to areas of shared responsibility.

KRAs agreed during appraisal:

1 Set goals and objectives.

2 Prioritize the person's activities and help improve their time/work management.

3 Assist in making value-added decisions.

4 Clarify department, team and individual roles.

5 Help the person to focus on results and not activities.

6 Align the person's role with the organization's business or strategic plans.

7 Communicate to others the person's job purpose.

KRAs for a position are its observable, measurable, value-adding outputs. They are the results that justify the existence of a job. So you should have agreed with the employee beforehand:

What is the team's mission and purpose?
What would not happen if the position disappeared?
What are the position's unique contributions?

Usually each KRA can be described in a few words. Positions typically have five or six KRAs. You will also have agreed with the employee their objectives for the year that you are now about to review. Objectives are specific statements of intended outcome. They need to define in detail what represents success for a core accountability. They represent the position's specific contribution to the departmental, team and organization goals. It's important that the objectives are SMART – specific, measurable, achievable, result-oriented and time bound. Typically there will be up to three SMART objectives for the most significant accountabilities, plus one personal development objective. There should also have been prioritizing of objectives, with regard to how much time and effort should be devoted to each objective. A good measure is to use A as critical and B as important.

With an established member of staff you should have reviewed the statement of objectives for the past year that were clarified in the appraisal form documentation. It's also important to think about the trends in performance or behaviour of the person you are to appraise, to see if there has been improvement (if that was required), or whether they still apply. Obviously if performance had not been up to standard, warning bells would have sounded and remedial action taken. If performance had been impacted by activities beyond the control of the appraisee, then this also will have been discussed informally and objectives renegotiated.

The person being reviewed should have had ample time to complete their part of the appraisal form. They will have reviewed how they achieved the objectives set during the previous review meeting. If they did not achieve all the objectives, they should come to the meeting with ideas on how this could be remedied. The form

---

Tips and techniques

Prior to the appraisal process

- The documentation for the appraisee should have been sent out well in advance, and the meeting time and venue indicated.
- Adequate time should have been allowed (90 minutes up to 3 hours).

- A quiet meeting room booked, and no interruptions should be allowed.

- As the appraiser, you should have reviewed the objectives for this person set in the last appraisal review, reviewed their job description, and thought through in what direction the department or team are going to move in the next year, and how this will impact on the job of the appraisee.

- Get to know about skills sets that the appraisee might have used out of the workplace, and consider how you might be able to use these within the working environment.

- Draft appropriate SMART objectives for the coming year.

- The scoring process should have been explained, and also the fact that it is there to prompt action.

- Set a clear agenda and stick to it. Should a new topic crop up that is not directly relevant to the review in hand, schedule another meeting for this.

will have also have asked them to give thought to training needs and requirements, and career aspirations.

Running the meeting itself

The overall atmosphere during the meeting should be positive and forward looking. Begin by handing out praise of some kind. Obviously if the appraisee has achieved a particular target this is in keeping. But even if they haven't, find something positive to say about how they have tackled the activity. For example, with someone in sales, if they have not met sales targets in volume or value terms, it may be possible to praise exemplary sales presentations and written proposals. How to remedy the situation and achieve targets should obviously be discussed, because this is the point of having a performance measure in place. Should the outcome be that the appraisee cannot take the appropriate steps to correct the situation, then a possible career alignment should be discussed – for example in the case mentioned above, a career focused on sales support or marketing.

If the person being appraised has done nothing particularly well, then praise is not in keeping, and you need to take stock of the situation and recommend appropriate action. It could be that the person is new to the role and a square peg in a round hole, and you should review other roles that might be more appropriate for them. Or maybe an able and well-respected long-term member of the team has been transferred into an unsuitable situation, and should be redeployed. Or perhaps family problems have interfered with work and consideration should be given to leave-of-absence or counselling.

Obviously individual cases require individual and sensitive handling in an atmosphere of trust and complete confidentiality, and both of you must recognize that an appraisal session is not appropriate for this level of discussion.

So working on the premise that the person has performed well, kick off the session with sincere praise for notable achievements, and then get the appraisee to review their performance by asking questions such as:

- What has given you particular satisfaction since your last review?
- How do you think you have performed against your last performance KRAs?
- What do you think were your best achievements?
- How would you rate your progress, and why, against agreed objectives?
- What examples can you give where you have lived our company's values and standards?
- What feedback examples (from customers, etc) can you relate?
- What personal strengths have helped you in your position?
- What concerns or obstacles, internal or external, have you encountered in accomplishing your job?

These questions give both parties an agreed picture of how the appraisee has evolved since the last session.

They may have tried doing a few new things, such as addressing a conference, giving a training course, or helping to plan or lead a project rather than just executing plans devised by others. If these rated high on the satisfaction/pleasure scale, you have measures of recent personal development and clues to future evolution.

The same applies if some long-term activity has metamorphosed from being a chore into being a source of delight.

Reviewing the past year from the manager's perspective

We all change with time, and during this part of the appraisal, the manager should have easy access to the notes made during previous sessions so as to spot trends. For example, many of us were very nervous the first time we addressed a large audience and probably hated the experience, but were forced by circumstances to try again and found it easier, and easier, and suddenly discovered that it is fun and a source of pleasure. A succession of meeting notes should make this clear and the organization has now gained a willing representative for the conference platform or classroom. Evolution at work!

Future planning

So now is the time to turn from the past and present towards the future. In general, since we tend to fear change, most of us will seek to continue doing our present job with some fine-tuning of the content or training so that we can do these better or specialize in the areas we do best. However, keep the discussion content flowing from the appraisee: Start with a selection of present-focused questions such as:

- What do you see as your professional strengths today?
- What opportunity does your current position provide if you reach your (medium- and longer-term) career expectations?

Through to future oriented questions:

- What areas or aspects of your work would you like to develop or improve by your next review?

- What tasks can you handle in the future?

- In which other areas can you improve your performance?

- What objectives would you like to set for yourself?

- What are the timescales for these?

- What do you see as your short-term goals and career interests (1–2 years)?

- What do you see as your long-term goals and career interests (2–5 years)?

- What actions can I/others take to help you accomplish your expectations?

- What are you going to do to accomplish your expectations? Within what timescale do you expect these to be attained?

- What training and development do you need in light of our jointly agreed objectives for next year?

Assuming that both you and the member of your team you are appraising expect the same relationship to continue, albeit with some evolution in the actual work content for the next period, you can move on to agree some concrete, measurable, win–win objectives. You should take the lead by asking questions such as, 'How shall we measure your performance against your targets?' and 'What will you achieve by X date?'

In this scenario, you will be mentally matching the appraisee's desires against team and corporate needs to ensure that the individual is able to make a positive contribution towards pre-established (even though changing) goals. It is also necessary to caution them against over-stretching themselves or underestimating their abilities, since both extremes are damaging to the individual and could be harmful to the organization. Eventually both parties should agree on sensible SMART objectives, write them down then put them in a safe place for a day or two.

It is easy get carried away by the euphoria generated by a happy and productive meeting, so it makes sense to allow those couple of days for personal review of what has been agreed. Is the target really too demanding? Arrange a few minutes to review the agreement in the cold light of a new day and then sign it or amend it before signature. Have a copy each, along with copies of any forms or minutes of the meeting, so that they are always available for reference and can, if need be, act as an objective basis on which to discuss divergence's between promise and outcome in the future.

Setting measurement of performance

So in setting performance standards there needs to be a measure in place. If we take the example of staff working in a sales environment what sort of measures could be put in place?

Using the formula

$$A - S = V$$

actual performance (A) is compared with a preset standard (S) and action is considered, and if necessary taken, by considering the variance (V) between the two.

A variety of standards can be used and these may relate to everything from the number of calls made in a day to the sales of a particular product. In nature they are:

Absolute standards: These are specific targets (eg annual sales revenue). They are important, but only provide certain information.

Moving standards: These look at results over time (eg a moving annual total) and thus highlight more about trends and likely outcome.

Diagnostic standards: As the name suggests these are designed to show the reasons why results are as they are.

In selling there are only four key variables: who is called on (the nature and type of customer or prospect), how many people are called on (more potential customers seen = potentially more sales), how often they are called on (call frequency) and – a whole separate area – what is done face to face with the customer (the quality and effectiveness of the sales approach).

The essence of measurement is change. The knowledge of what is happening allows action to be taken either aiming to bring things back on track if there is a shortfall, or to build on success. This last point is key. Measurement or another word for it is control is not simply to correct faults. It is to accentuate the positive. It is just as useful to see a positive variance, ask why this should be happening and build on the action that is creating it. Sales manager have the remit to provide a framework and encourage discipline among salespeople, however, their prime job is to act as a catalyst to success. By viewing measurement as both focusing on positive and negative results and acting as a spur to change, its value will be maximised.

Looking at other industry sectors, what might be measured? In IT there could be:

- operational targets – measuring the amount of downtime with IT equipment;
- number of key projects to deliver/upgrades;
- user satisfaction targets;
- projects running on time – do we deliver what we promise?

In the media section there could be:

- customer service levels;
- effectiveness of advertising and marketing systems;
- distribution channels – how effective are they at getting products and services to market?
- the forms of communication that our target audience are most susceptible to;

Accommodating differences and change of circumstances

Throughout the last section there was an underlying assumption that the period following the appraisal would be pretty similar to the period preceding it. The team's objectives would remain much the same, the same manager–team member relationship would continue, and the latter would carry on making much the same contribution. Very often this is the case. However, there are a variety of factors that can change this assumption and if we are to be realistic we should consider some other cases.

Let's say this person is valued for their present and potential contributions to the team and you wish to keep them in your team. Since the appraisal is specifically designed to be centred around the appraisee, what negatives or divergences might emerge?

Here are some examples of what they might say:

'My personal circumstances have changed and I need to spend more time with my family. As much as I enjoy business travel, I want less of it (or the opposite).'

'Thank you for saying I am a good marketing executive, but I am getting bored with some aspects of the task; I want to move towards x/y/z...'

'It has been great working in the field/headquarters, but now I want to gain experience in headquarters/the field.'

'I have had a great time working here, but I (or my partner) feel that this would be a good time for an assignment in another country (or to go home).'

'I consider that I am good at my current job, but think I am ready to move to a more senior position.'

The appraisee is not unhappy, but feels that the time has come to plan for change, either to evolve their career, or to take account of events or pressures from outside the workplace.

Now we have come so far in a very positive atmosphere, so we must continue this way, even though, as a manager, you may be disappointed or hurt by what may seem like rejection from the person you are appraising. Two observations may help you deal with this. Firstly, we all went through the same developmental process as we outgrew a succession of jobs in our own pasts. We didn't in some way reject or even criticize a previous manager who had helped us grow until we reached the stage of wishing to move on; personal change and growth is natural. Secondly, as a manager you have two roles: you run your team, but you are also a representative of the organization as a whole; when conducting an appraisal you are in part seeking to promote the health and wealth of the entire organization, even at a short-term cost to your own team.

Now it is obvious that in most cases you will not be able in the short term to do more than accept the inputs and promise (sincerely) to do whatever you can to accommodate the wishes of this person. That is sufficient. You then have to carry out your promise and, if necessary in consultation with the HR department and managers running other departments, plot out some possibilities for discussion with the appraisee at a continuation of the session.

Changes in the organization may well be emerging, and it's up to you to take the lead in implementing them. For example:

'The company has set up a local sales or support organization in country X, so we don't need to keep flying you to and fro (or we want to set up an organization in X and need people on temporary assignment to get it going).'

'The ranges of services and support facilities are evolving and we need to build up expertise on the new and de-emphasize the old.'

'We are refocusing our approach to the market and need people to help manage the transition.'

'Our team has established a best-practice approach in a particular area of activity, and we need to make others aware of it.'

'Some other department or team needs our expertise to help them.'

As a result of this corporate evolution there may be new opportunities you should bring to the attention of the appraisee, showing how their expertise could bring greater value to the organization by working on a different stage.

Or the news may not be positive, such as the department or a team is to be run down, or their job is to be phased out. If this is the case, you need to have explored all possible options for re-deployment of this person with your manager plus consulted with your HR department well in advance of the appraisal meeting, so that you can discuss the appropriate way forward during the review.

After the meeting

Some difficulties may occur, but the overall feeling and outcome should always be constructive. If individual weaknesses are identified they will need addressing. If changes demand personal development, then priorities must be set and action implemented. If new roles or responsibilities are agreed, they will need formalizing. Experience shows that only a poor, or unusual, appraisal does not produce useful action for the future – and how many new ideas are needed to justify the time taken?

Despite other pressures, the worst possible outcome is for an appraisal to set something useful in train, but not follow it through; so always record and follow through decisions. Even the best performances can be improved. Even the most expert and competent people have new things to learn and ways to adopt; the present dynamic work environment sees to that. The appraisal process is *not* all about criticism and highlighting errors or faults (though realistically there may be some of this). It is about using analysis and discussion to move forward. It is about building on success, sharing good experience and effective approaches and, above all, it is about making more of the future.

And if you, and your people, are not there to affect the future, what are you there for?

CASE STUDY

Table 7.1 A leading telecoms performance management cycle

Component	Timing	Outputs
Objective setting – KRAs and work objectives	Beginning of year and/or on new appointment and/or on changing business needs	Set of agreed KRAs, objectives, measurement methods and timelines
Definition of competency Requirements for role	Beginning of year and/or on new appointment and/or on changing business needs	Set of agreed competency requirements, measurement methods and timelines
Development planning	Beginning of year and/or on new appointment and/or on changing business needs	Agreed development plan based on development themes arising from competencies requirements for role
Career planning	Beginning of year, or as agreed between line manager and individual	Agreed action plan aligned to organizational objectives to deliver on career development needs
Ongoing feedback	Regularly throughout the performance cycle on a formal and informal basis. Objectives should be reviewed to ensure they are on schedule	Amendments to objectives if appropriate. Agreement on remedial action if necessary
Formal quarterly and mid-year reviews	Every three months during the performance cycle	Feedback on performance to date. If appropriate, agreement on revised objectives and action plans for remedial action

(continued)

Table 7.1 *(Continued)*

Component	Timing	Outputs
Formal year end review	At the end of the performance cycle or on appointment to a new role with new objectives	Agreement on a rating based on performance during the cycle. Agreement on development actions to be encompassed into development plan for year ahead. Review of career plan and agreement on future actions. Detailed performance improvement. Action plan if marginal performer

Key tasks

- Consider whether you have you got the balance right in your team between tasks and people.

- Use the appraisal process to *re*-recruit and *re*-motivate team members.

- Control any eagerness to judge. Let team members evaluate themselves first before giving your opinion. After all, whose opinions do we all prefer most?

- Review your questioning techniques for the annual performance and development review scheme to ensure that they clarify the past, present and future.

- Take as long as it takes for each appraisal. You can't do it justice in one hour!

- Consider using 360° feedback as part of your appraisal approach.

08

Recognition and rewarding performance

Introduction

Organizational reward schemes need to be developed around key business drivers through team and individual development. So reward schemes need to place emphasis on moving away from protectionism to collaboration, from passing problems up the organization to solving them directly, from focusing on the number of units produced in a time period to meeting the needs of the customer. This is a shift from status to results. People observe what is being discussed, recognized and rewarded, what is punished, tolerated and also ignored. So it is up to you to make sure that recognition and reward is pertinent and underpins the environment you wish to create.

Consider your own business. What kind of performance is rewarded and how? It's obviously essential to choose rewards that are appropriate in your organization and possible within its structures. A good manager will reward their staff and build on their strengths. As higher performance levels are achieved, it is important to set new targets and new challenges. Reward systems will always need to be reviewed and updated and fresher and new approaches be found.

The choice might be a celebration for the whole team. Maybe it would be a reward for service delivery – once a month. Some people want a financial incentive for profits and company gains.

Everyone has a different expectation of reward and recognition. The common factor is that people want some kind of acknowledgement. Most businesses link rewards to key performance indicators (KPIs). Achieve them and get a reward. Achieve beyond expectations and get a bigger reward! Some companies are very creative with their rewards, for example giving people a chance to give back to the community during company time.

Rewarding performance

People often resist change for reasons that make good sense to them, even if those reasons don't correspond to organizational goals. So it is crucial to recognize, reward, and celebrate accomplishments.

Rosebeth Moss Kanter

Moving on to assessing the performance of an individual, rewarding them appropriately should be based on not only *what* has been achieved, but also *how* it has been achieved. Has it been consistent with the values of the organization, its code of conduct and ethics, and any other policies and standards that have been used as a benchmark during the appraisal process? Many organizations use a five-point rating, moving from the lowest rating 'unacceptable' to 'far exceeding required high standards'.

At the end of the appraisal you need to consider whether the appraisee has achieved results in their current role. If they have been offered training and support, and they have not delivered against an agreed standard, then you are unlikely to consider rewarding performance, or believe they are able to cope with more, and promotion and new opportunities may – rightly – elude them until performance improves.

For those that have achieved a satisfactory or above (up to the top) grading there is usually a scaled bonus/incentive or reward scheme in place. The classic rewards include performance-related pay, bonuses, and sometimes inclusion in an enhanced health care scheme or pension plan. These are controlled by your organization's policies/HR department if you have one, unless you are an owner of an SME without an HR department, and then you would be the decision maker.

My own view of reward schemes is that organizations should establish a flexible approach to pay management in terms of each business and individual. This means that pay and bonus awards should favour high performers and the responsibility for pay and bonus decisions should rest with the line manager. Pay systems – like all systems – should be simplified and transparent. This means, your team members should have a complete understanding of their total package. A best-practice approach to reward says that:

- A 'one size fits all' approach must go.
- Pay systems should be open, predictable and designed to demonstrate links to performance.
- They should be designed to recognize individual, team, and group performance.
- Reward according to a person's ability to create value.
- Build managers capability to take responsibility for managing reward.

When I worked at the Europe Japan Centre our research department did a good deal of research into pay award schemes. One of the findings that consistently came through was that people wanted pay tied to performance. Another finding was that employees wanted people to be fired for not performing. In fact, failure to discipline and fire non-performers was one of the most demotivating actions an organization could take – or fail to take. It would rank on the top of the finding list next to paying poor performers the same wage as performers.

CASE STUDY   Examples of SMEs health giving benefits packages

- Australian law firm Seyfarth Shaw offers a mindfulness room where you can meditate, take part in health and well-being seminars, have an occasional massage and learn how to make smoothies.

- The 7 Stars media agency in London have free Boris bike keys so staff can get between meetings in a health-enhancing way. They also offer free fruit and breakfast bars and every employee gets free private health care. They also have various sporting activities organized such as football, netball, yoga and Pilates. Any of these benefits can be swapped for a more tailored benefit such as dental insurance.

- Genentech, the San Francisco bio tech firm, offers an on-site farmers' market.

... and financial incentives

- Reassured Ltd based in Alton, Hampshire, who have 70 staff (in 2016), are a brokerage firm for various types of insurance. They introduced a shares scheme in 2013 for all employees regardless of level of seniority. There are currently 34 shareholders within the business and the MD has given away 5 per cent of the company to them.

... plus giving something back

- The Jenrick Recruitment Group is based in the UK. It believes in the principle of giving something back to the community. The company donates in excess of £2,000 per year to charitable causes nominated by staff and the local community.

So this is one type of flexibility. Another form of flexibility that you can offer, and in my experience this is one of the most successful reward devices (short of money), is flexitime – deciding on the times a person starts and leaves for the day. Of course you have to have cover within your team, and this needs to be jointly agreed. Another option is to allow a person a day off without it being deducted from their holiday allowance. Everyone has a personal life that needs to be taken care of – going to school sports days, seeing a doctor/dentist/mortgage adviser. As long as the person deserves the reward, and doesn't abuse the system and take too many days without permission, why not? Make sure this reward is seen to be fairly and equitably balanced by all members of your team.

Moving on, let's look at what else you can use as part of the reward system, even if there is little or no funding available. You can offer:

- job enlargement or enrichment;
- career development;
- personal skill development.

Rewarding performance when no funds are available

It is a fact of life that during these tough economic times funds are not always available for rewarding staff. So what options do you have when there is little or no budget available?

Think of what a business developer does when they go out to meet a client. They ask questions to find out the needs of the client. Well it's no different in this situation. You have to find out what your people need to be more satisfied with their job, and what might re-energize and stimulate them and keep them as active participating members of your team.

Getting to know the needs of your team

You need to think laterally and creatively. Firstly, bear in mind there will be a range of different personalities in your team, who will be motivated in different ways. Find out what excites and makes each person tick. What 'lights their fire'? Talk to them and listen (make sure they do most of the talking). They will tell you what they like and don't like about their current and previous work responsibilities. So this could be on the positive side, that they enjoy working on x type of project, or with y team or that they want more individual projects to do where they can problem solve on their own, developing a resolution from start to finish. On the negative side they might say that they find a procedure, or excessive rules and regulations that are currently in place, too restrictive. Now inevitably certain rules/regulations/procedures are there for a purpose. It could be they relate to achieving a regulatory performance standard, or are there for legal or health and safety purposes. These need to stay. However, as part of the continuous improvement process, it is important to challenge the status quo to make sure processes, procedures and standards are there ultimately to enhance performance, not keep it in a straightjacket.

Once you know what is important to each person, link this interest to your business needs. On some occasions this will be a straightforward exchange of information. On other occasions you have to 'sell' the concept of their work being expanded or changed in some way. As a rule of thumb, when employees find jobs exciting, challenging and interesting they do better. So bear this in mind to make assignments more meaningful. In what way? Through *job enrichment* or *job enlargement*.

Job enrichment is the addition to a job of tasks that increases the amount of employee control or responsibility. It is a vertical expansion of the job as opposed to a horizontal expansion of a job, which is called job enlargement.

A brief word about job enlargement. This is a process that increases the scope of the job through extending the range of its duties and responsibilities. In the manufacturing environment it can take away the monotony of doing just one task repeatedly. For example, instead of building just one component part of a humidifier, a team builds the entire product from start to finish. It's important to ensure that the employee can see how their work affects others. In enlarging a job you need to make sure you are giving more responsibility and more variety, not just more work. So how do you 'sell' the concept of job enrichment? By saying that better performance might lead to:

- an opportunity to work in a different office/be transferred to the international division or more autonomy in performing assignments;
- work on an assignment that the person has indicated they are keen to work on;
- work with a different group;
- more varied duties.

Of course, what you have to bear in mind is that before you even talk about job enrichment or enlargement you make sure that the current working conditions, ie how employees are supervised/facilitated, what is expected of them, are to a mutually agreed standard. If this part of your relationship with the person or team you wish to reward for good performance is not as it should be, then any attempts to increase satisfaction are likely to be sterile.

> 'Far and away the best prize life offers is the chance to work hard at work worth doing.'
>
> Theodore Roosevelt

Job enrichment

Job enrichment can apply to individual jobs or to autonomous work groups. But in either case the objective is to give people more freedom and autonomy in the organization of their work. This concept was originally promoted by Frederick Herzberg in his 1968 article entitled 'One More Time: How do you motivate employees?'

Hackman and Oldman (1976: 250) identified five factors of job design that typically contribute to people's enjoyment of a job:

1 Skill variety – increasing the number of skills that individuals use while performing work.

2 Task identity – enabling people to perform a job from start to finish.

3 Task significance – providing work that has a direct impact on the organization or its stakeholders.

4 Autonomy – increasing the degree of decision making, and the freedom to choose how and when work is done.

5 Feedback – increasing the amount of recognition for doing a job well, and communicating the results of people's work.

There are clearly advantages to an individual or team being given the choice and freedom to plan, execute and evaluate a project or task. From the company's perspective it can ultimately reduce staff turnover and absenteeism, and they will have gained personnel with more skills sets and adaptability.

On the negative side there could be higher costs in terms of installing a new system – be it equipment or machinery. There is also the dip in productivity should people be involved in reskilling, undertaking training of some kind. There could also be increased salary costs as people's job description changes and they move into a different grading band. There can also be resentment and conflict caused by a team being given more autonomy. I have seen this at first hand when we introduced a self-managed team into a packaging line in a pharmaceutical organization. The team themselves were really fired up and set themselves even tougher targets than they would have been set by management in the past. Once the autonomous team was up and running, the down time of the production line reduced significantly, and productivity shot through the roof. From the start of this pilot initiative there was back-stabbing gossip in the canteen and resentment by non-enabled/empowered teams, based on the premise that this particular team where being given special privileges, etc. Once the pilot initiative proved to be successful, the whole process was rolled out across the packaging department; however, both management and those in the team needed to keep their nerve and positive attitude during the trial process.

Undoubtedly, job enrichment has more pluses than minuses. When I have spoken to people in companies during research assignments, they have made complimentary comments about having their job enriched.

'I had reached a career plateau, and had become bored with the routine nature of my job. Once I was given the opportunity to work on a task force to see how we could improve our customer retention rate I felt invigorated and time in the day just flew by. I enjoyed meeting people from other departments, and finding out far more about how we go to market.'

'I have moved on now from just being a researcher, and been able to specialize in web base design, which is my passion. We are a small business unit, and of course when a new research project comes in I go back to being purely a researcher, but know that ultimately when I look to relocate to New Zealand I will have this new skill set which can help me redirect my career.'

People also commented favourably not only about developing new skills, but also about creating new business networks, and finding out for themselves that they could think far more creatively than they imagined was possible in the past.

On the minus side, I have heard comments about how difficult some people have found it to balance their current workload with taking on new responsibilities. Another issue that has been raised is lack of clarity of information when being given a new 'enriching' assignment. 'I felt I was just thrown in the deep end, and it was a sink or swim scenario.' So all of this comes down to keeping the communication channels open between all/both parties, for the manager to give crystal clear instructions to start off with, and both parties giving feedback to each other throughout. There is also a need to be pragmatic in approach and help people to self-analyse priorities. In turn give them access to you as their manager, should they be unclear about any part of their new workload.

So looking at a staged approach to implementing job enrichment with an individual:

Step 1: Find out what part of the job a person particularly enjoys, and what part of their workload they would prefer to reduce. There is no point in enriching part of a workload that they do not enjoy.

Step 2: You need to balance operational needs with job satisfaction, so think of the range of skills and competencies you have in your team, and assess how feasible it would be to incorporate the person's expressed needs and requirements. You probably don't want to have to redesign your entire work process for one individual, unless it's of benefit to productivity and is fair to the whole team.

Step 3: Make the changes, and let everyone know what you are doing and why. Remember to monitor your efforts, and regularly evaluate the changes and how effective they have been not only for the good of the person concerned, but also for the good of the team.

Job rotation

Another option that you have for enrichment is job rotation. This involves moving an employee through a variety of jobs within the organization. From an employer's point of view this can be costly, as employees usually need to retrain, but from the latter's point of view it can be rewarding, and morale boosting. It will also give them a far greater understanding of how the whole organization works, which can go a good way towards breaking down interpersonal and inter-departmental barriers which inevitably develop in organizations. Japanese companies that have adopted the principles of Kaizen (continuous improvement) make a point of using this motivational methodology. Staff can work for protracted periods of time – a year or two, for example – in a different department to the one they were recruited for in the first place.

Group job enrichment

Ultimate job enrichment for a team is for them to become self-sufficient and autonomous through job redesign. Job redesign focuses on combining existing jobs, forming work groups, and/or allowing closer contact between employees and individual suppliers or customers.

As we have explored in Chapter 3, there is a defined sequence to delegating projects and tasks, and you cannot do this in one go. You need to be actively involved with the group to start off with, facilitating most activities, and then gradually relinquish control until they make all their own decisions about scheduling, linking with suppliers for materials, rest breaks, and evaluation processes/ quality control. They could even select people to join the team. Your main purpose is to give them a goal to achieve, be there in a supportive capacity, and help them link with internal customers should the need arise.

There is a further option that can be used – breaking down your typical functional lines and forming them into project-focused units. For example, rather than having all of your marketing people in one department, with team leaders/supervisors directing who works on which project, you can split the department into specialized project units – so specific storyboard creators, copywriters and designers (say) could all work together for one client or one campaign. This is an excellent way to build autonomy, and build client relationships.

CASE STUDY Let's Go Holdings

Let's Go Holdings is a London-based group of brand advocacy specialists in the tech and media space.

Its founder and CEO, Callum Negus-Fancy, left school at 17 without taking his A levels, setting up his initial company in 2008. He identified a gap in the market: no one was creating the rave experience for 16- to 18-year-olds. He was cautious about spend, and used a direct selling technique getting people to sell tickets to their friends on a commission basis, so that he could pay for both the bands and the venue without needing to seek start-up capital.

He learnt from this initial experience and expanded his business in 2011 and 2013 creating a branding company, Your Vine, and Physical

Networks, which focuses on selling person-to person-festive tickets. Since this early acorn of a business he has now managed to raise £4 million from investors, the holding company has a turnover of £5.5M and it employs 70 staff (*MoneyWeek* magazine, 22.1.15).

He is a firm believer in giving his staff both autonomy and accountability, and creating a work–life balance that works for them. He puts this philosophy into practice by using ROWE – the Results Only Work Environment (Jody Thompson and Cali Ressler). So what does this approach mean in practice? Each person can work wherever they want, whenever they want, as long as they meet agreed objectives. This means that they are crystal-clear about what their measurable results are and managers manage the work not the people. When Callum put this in to practice he asked employees to come up with their own metrics for measurement purposes. He asked them a simple question: 'What would go wrong if you weren't there?' This is then what should be measured – focusing on the few things that matter rather than the minor details.

His philosophy has been that in order to grow his company strategically and rapidly he needs to attract top creative talent. These people are in demand, so how can you not only initially attract them but retain their services? By offering the opportunity for a good work–life balance and tapping in to their intrinsic motivation. He believes that asking people to be 9–5 attendees at work and using time as a metric does not necessarily produce the most productive environment. Of course, having an office base offers equipment, a place to meet work colleagues and a sense of belonging.

Other organizations that have adopted ROWE are Gap, the US retailer, Spinweb, the Department of Transportation and the American Soceity of Clinical Oncology.

Meet the Boss TV

I believe ROWE works particularly well during the initial growth stage of a company through until it becomes a medium-sized business. It can also be introduced when dealing with projects when individuals report directly into the head of the business. These type of projects are often found in businesses that are diversifying and introduce new income streams or ventures as they offer a lower-risk lower-cost alternative to the use of existing staff or the need to bring in a whole new team of employees.

Is a reward always necessary?

Everything we have explored in this chapter so far has been based on the premise that you have assessed through conversations with the various individuals that they have a need to expand their horizons, and take on more challenging and mind-expanding activities for enrichment purposes.

The ultimate idea is to improve the quality of life for an employee, so they are motivated to accomplish more. However, in order for a job to be enriched the employee has to have the desire to accept new ways of accomplishing tasks. Some employees lack the skills and knowledge required to perform enriched jobs, or even the volition to do more. They enjoy doing routine work because it is stress free and they are in their comfort zone. I can remember having a member of my team like this. She was a great 'completer and finisher' (as in Belbin's *Team Roles*), and also an invaluable member of the team. Being a consultant I often have to create sizeable proposals/discussion documents for clients, which could include graphics, visuals and detailed diagrams. I wouldn't always have the time or knowledge myself to create a multifaceted visual. She had a good creative eye, and also knew how to use IT packages to create wonderful visuals, just from a verbal description of what I was looking for. She had worked in a management development unit for years and certainly could have expanded her personal knowledge in a variety of ways, but she simply didn't want to. She enjoyed doing organizational administration work, tidying up copy in a proposal so that it all aligned, and creating visuals. She simply did not want to do more, even though I encouraged her to 'think out of the box'.

There is another category of staff that is worth looking at. They do not necessarily want financial reward, or job enrichment – these are *achievement-motivated people*.

Achievement-motivated staff

Accel – Team Development have undertaken some research through David McClelland from Harvard University. For over twenty years he has studied and perceived that some people have an intense need to achieve, and others, perhaps the majority, do not seem to be as concerned about achievement as others. McClelland's research led him to believe that the need for achievement is a distinct human motive that can be distinguished from other needs. More important, the achievement motive can be isolated and assessed in any group. From his research experiments he came to realize that people with a high need for achievement would set themselves moderately difficult but potentially achievable goals. They would only behave like this if they could influence the outcome. Achievement-motivated people are not gamblers. They prefer to work on a problem rather than leave the outcome to chance.

So, as a manager dealing with achievement-motivated staff, you need, for example, to give them a moderately challenging problem to resolve, with a moderate degree of risk, because they would feel their abilities and effort will probably influence the outcome. This type of person seems to be more concerned with personal achievement than financial reward. They don't reject the reward but it is not as essential as the accomplishment itself. Money to these people is valuable primarily as a measure of their performance. Another characteristic is that they need feedback and information about their work. They are not so interested in personal characteristics such as being helpful or cooperative. You find this type of person as an entrepreneur or in sales. McClelland believes these people get ahead because they spend a great deal of time thinking about how things might be improved.

The interesting thing about an achievement-motivated person is that they get ahead because of getting things done themselves, but when they are promoted and the outcome depends not only on their own work but also that of others they may be less effective. So if you have an achievement-motivated member in your team, play to their strengths. If you are in the process of succession planning, however, you will need to analyse their potential managerial acteristics in more depth, and create a personal development plan for them to bridge the skills and competency gaps.

Relating this back to Herzberg, achievement-motivated people tend to be attracted by the 'motivators' (the job itself).

So to summarize the chapter so far, in considering any form of reward system you have to understand the needs of each individual who reports to you. Will job enrichment or enlargement be appropriate, or should you bear in mind that a person is perfectly happy in their role as it stands? Have you got achievement-motivated staff, and if so are you setting them moderately challenging problems to resolve, or assignments to undertake where they have a good chance of achieving their goals?

And in terms of showing people your appreciation with their involvement and effort, what else can you do?

Tips and techniques

Showing appreciation and building a feel-good factor

1 **Link them with others:** Introduce members of your team to key suppliers, or customers, or their telephone contact at another office whom they normally would not meet on a face-to-face basis.

2 **Reward effort as well as success:** Not all ideas that get proposed can be taken forward. But you want to encourage ideas for improvement from your team. Give a small gift on an annual basis for the person who comes up with the most ideas – however zany.

3 **Send a hand-written note thanking the team or an individual** from you as the CEO/manager.

4 **Create laughter:** On a dress-down Friday get members of your team to bring in pictures of themselves as a baby, and get everyone to guess who is who.

5 **Acknowledge special effort:** A group of employees at Unipart decided to give up part of their holiday leave to reconfigure the layout of equipment on the shop floor. This ultimately produced great cost savings for the company. The senior management team hired a local venue, and asked the team to make a presentation on stage as to why and how they decided to revise the layout of equipment. All the senior management were in the audience during the presentation.

6 **Create a special leaving gift:** If somebody is going to leave your team and has performed particularly well, get everyone in the team to put together a small album charting the projects you have all worked on together, including the outcomes. In turn each member of the team could write their own personal message to the leaver, highlighting special times that they had worked together, including feelings and thoughts that they had shared.

7 **Offer choice:** Give a high-performing individual the choice of which projects to work on.

8 **Create a high-achievers wall:** Put up a pinboard in a public area within the company. On a monthly basis put a picture of the employee who has been voted by their team or department as worthy of special notice. Underneath the picture have a brief description of why they have been elected as employee of the month.

And finally, from *The Manager's Book of Decencies: Small gestures build great companies* by Steve Harrison, a couple of ideas:

9 **Celebrate birthdays:** Cisco Systems Inc's CEO John Chambers hosts an hour-long birthday breakfast for any employees with a birthday in that month. Employees are invited to ask him anything. They feel recognized, and he gains loyal employees who share their ideas.

10 **Coffee time:** During the busiest times of the year executives at the Cigna Group push around the coffee carts, serving drinks and refreshments to their colleagues. As they serve, executives talk to staff, getting ideas and finding out about client feedback, both good and bad.

Showing appreciation is fine, but what changes have organizations made recently in pay and conditions when the going has got seriously tough? These are some topical strategies that were implemented in the 2008–10 downturn, with some success.

Case examples of changes to pay and conditions that companies have made in tough times

- **Introduce a shorter working week:** This in effect is spreading the same amount of work around more people as a way to reduce the number of employees being 'let go'. In March 2009 workers at Jaguar Land Rover's manufacturing operations in Castle Bromwich and Halewood switched to a four-day week in exchange for the company's agreement that there would not be any compulsory redundancies for two years.

- **Freeze pay:** ITV, the broadcaster, froze pay for its senior employees earning over £60,000 a year in February 2009, in light of fast-falling advertising revenues. A below-inflation pay rise was imposed on full-time employees earning more than £25,000.

- **Cut pay:** A study by the British Chambers of Commerce (BCC) carried out in April 2009 revealed that for their sample of 400 companies 12 per cent were planning to cut pay. In October 2008 some 2,500 staff based at seven different JCB factories voted to take a £50-a-week pay cut and work a four-day week in order to prevent 350 colleagues losing their jobs. In June 2009 British Airways (BA) persuaded 6,940 of its 40,000 employees to volunteer for unpaid leave, part-time working or unpaid work, saving the company up to £10 million.

- **Sell holidays to the staff:** Acco Brands Europe, the office supply firm, launched a holiday purchase scheme for its 500 UK employees in February 2009. Employees can buy between two and 10 extra days' holiday per year, on top of their normal annual leave. The benefit is offered via salary sacrifice, so employees save on tax and National Insurance contributions (NICs) and Acco makes savings of up to 12.8 per cent on NICs, in addition to cutting payroll costs. A pilot scheme produced savings of £37,964 in payroll costs for the company in one quarter.

- **Offer shares in lieu of pay:** In June 2009 British Airways (BA) pilots voted on a deal taking a pay cut in exchange for company shares, in order to cut payroll costs at the airline. The pilots took a wage cut of 2.61 per cent on their basic pay as well as a 20 per cent cut in flying-time allowances. These changes will generate £26 million of annual savings for BA, in exchange for which the pilots were given BA shares worth £13 million if certain company targets are achieved. The pilots have to hold these shares for three years, until June 2014, after which they can sell or hold onto them as they wish.

- **Reduce pension benefits:** In July 2009 Marks & Spencer announced changes to its final-salary pension scheme and early retirement arrangements in a bid to cut operating costs by between £175m and £200m. Annual increases in pensionable pay for the 21,000 active members of the final-salary pension scheme was capped at 1 per cent, whilst those who joined the pension scheme before 1996 also face reduced early retirement benefits.

We now move on to two other areas of activity that will have been discussed during the appraisal process – career development and personal skill development.

Career development

Organizations can vary in the approaches they adopt for career development of staff, like Barclays Bank or Homes for Islington, for example, which use their own competency model. These organizations' competencies framework forms the platform on which career management is built, and underpins all their people strategies, from reward through to career and personal development. We mentioned an example of a competency framework in Chapter 4, about staff recruitment. One way or another you would need to have a framework in place to aid both you and the person you are appraising to assess how they might develop their career.

In practical terms, how can you help the appraisee to think through how they might want to progress their career? Any agreement on a career plan needs to align performance objectives and organizational needs.

You need to get them to move on from purely technical to leadership and managerial competencies that are of significance, which will be assessed once they wish to progress. For example, get them to:

- **Assess their broader skills:** This could be anything from communication, problem solving, making presentations, through to managing people or projects.

- **Analyse their strengths and weaknesses:** This could include the number of years' work experience in a particular area, their education/training, talents and abilities, technical knowledge and personal characteristics.

- **Assess their work values:** Here they could consider factors such as having a:

  - strong need to achieve;
  - need for a high salary;
  - high job satisfaction requirement;
  - liking for doing something 'worthwhile';
  - desire to be creative, travel or be independent;
  - desire to continue working as part of your team, or any team for that matter!

- **Assess their personal characteristics:** Are they a risk taker, an innovator, or able to work under pressure, and how do such characteristics affect their work situation? Another consideration is to discuss if they prefer working independently on a particular aspect of any assignment. If they can add value through their contribution to the team effort, but shy away from group participation, then the people management route is not for them.

- **Assess their non-work characteristics:** Factors like family commitments, where they want to live and their attitude to time spent away from home.

- **Match their analysis to the market demands:** Consider realistically how well their overall capabilities and characteristics fit market opportunities.

With this clear, you can then jointly set defined objectives; the old adage 'if you do not know where you are going any road will do' is nowhere more true.

The next step is to encourage them to aim high. They can always look to trade down, but they should not miss out because they did not attempt it.

Personal skill development

Skill and competency development can be undertaken in a variety of ways, from self-learning (knowledge portals or the intranet/internet), experiential leaning, 'sitting with Nelly' or job rotation, through to guidance, for example being coached or having a mentor, or formal training courses. Help on using these different learning and development methodologies can be found in Chapter 9.

The important factor is to ensure that you monitor and measure the effectiveness of the approach being used. There is no point having someone sitting at a PC with an interactive training package, and believing they have gained an understanding of a topic, only to find out two or three weeks later, they can't remember anything they have been taught!

Key tasks

- Re-evaluate how you might reward staff when little or no budget is available. What form of job enlargement/enrichment can you offer?

- What might you have to consider if times are really tough, in terms of a more flexible working arrangement for staff? Meet with the unions or pertinent personnel in your organization.

- Have you got high-achievement motivated individuals, and are they being catered for appropriately?

- With regard to career planning, have you discussed with members of your team short (one-year) and projected long-term plans for their career development?

- How are you monitoring your teams learning and development? Have you set up a development plan that is SMART?

09

Creating a learning environment

Introduction

When you think back to your school/university days, the term 'learning' doesn't necessarily bring back the happiest of memories. Gaining an understanding of a topic was often done by rote, taught by teachers or tutors reading from a book, with few visual aids or activities to stimulate your imagination. The information didn't relate to the real world in which we operate.

The term 'learning' within organizations has now taken on a totally different meaning. The business world is no longer labour, material or energy intensive. It's knowledge intensive. The old organizational model, 'the top thinks and the local acts', has moved on to the concept of integrating thinking and acting at all levels. This shift to a knowledge-based society was identified way back in the 1960s by Peter Drucker. From this time onwards management thinkers have been producing academic research on how individuals and organizations learn.

The leading authority on the development of the 'learning environment' is Peter Senge, Head of the Center for Organizational Learning at the Massachusetts Institute of Technology, and author of the best-selling book *The Fifth Discipline* (1990). In brief, Senge argues that people who are keen to learn should embrace five disciplines:

1 Team learning.
2 Shared visions.

3 Mental models.

4 Personal mastery.

5 Systems thinking.

They should put aside their old 'memory models', learn to be open with others ('personal mastery'), understand how their organization really works ('systems thinking'), agree on a 'shared vision' and then work together to achieve a common purpose ('team learning').

Taking an example, the Apple Japan organization adopted this approach. Team meetings were already in place, but the time frame was expanded to get everyone's input and also allow time for 'team learning'. 'Personal mastery' was addressed by getting managers to set their staff challenging but reasonable goals. Adopting 'systems thinking' enabled each employee to make decisions taking the whole system into account instead of just focusing on their own problems.

No learning organization is built overnight. Success comes from carefully cultivated attitudes, commitments and management processes that accrue slowly and steadily. This involves learning how to handle people who possess knowledge. People can have knowledge at all levels, from factory-floor workers through to IT specialists, lawyers, scientists and doctors. It is obviously possible to fast-track the collection of information through technology, but this is not enough. Getting people to share their ideas and to think more expansively and creatively is the challenge.

So let's explore how this can be achieved. We will start by looking at how in practical terms learning manifests itself within an organization; this will be followed by how to create a learning and development strategy, planning for the development of your reports, and the learning and development resources that are available for you to take action.

How 'learning' manifests itself in an organization

- There is a commitment from the top for learning and personal development.

- There is ongoing analysis and awareness of marketplace developments and the competition.

- People are all levels are encouraged to 'think out of the box' and be creative – plus time and resources are allocated for them to do this.

- There is systematic problem solving, experimenting with new approaches, learning from past experience, and best-practice approaches of others.

- There is a free exchange and flow of information company-wide, aided by the appropriate technology.

- Cross-functional activities are encouraged, individuals create networks for support, and systems are in place to ensure that expertise is available where it is needed.

Use the word 'learning' and 'development' rather than the word 'training'. Why is this? The first two words put the emphasis on growth and determination – in other words, growing from within. The word 'training' implies putting skills into a person by prescribed training methods – which is less likely to enthuse and motivate people.

CASE STUDY   Periscopix

This digital marketing agency is featured in the *Sunday Times* Best SME Companies to Work For in 2015. The company help clients such as EMAP, Tesco and Toys R Us run online advertising campaigns. The average age of employees is 27. One of its strengths highlighted in the feedback research was the fact that the company promotes personal growth. Most staff with at least a year's experience are involved in training others in business essentials such as pay-per-click, Google Analytics and programmatic display (using software to buy adverts).

All experienced employees are encouraged to get involved with staff training. Mentoring is taken seriously, with the company offering staff a coach and guide to help them with technical on-the-job training, career advice and helping them to learn the company's best-practice policy.

Creating a (departmental or team) learning and development plan

As we mentioned above, there needs to be a commitment from the top for learning and personal development. Many organizations have their own learning and development function. Others do not. If you belong to the latter, what can you do if you wish to develop your staff and create a learning environment? What are some fundamental concepts that have proven to work elsewhere?

Besides being understood by those in your company, the purpose of learning and/or creating a learning environment is about managing gaps in:

- performance standards (learning needed for a current task or job);
- growth gaps (learning needed to achieve career goals);
- opportunity gaps (learning needed to qualify for an identified new job or role).

Your mission might be to create and *maximize value through developing your team's capabilities at lowest cost,* while your learning vision might to be known as *a team of employee choice.*

'Maximizing value' is one of those catch-all phrases. It means and totally depends upon:

- **Correctly diagnosing department/team training needs:** Creating and putting into effect learning interventions that align with organizational strategies and support value creation, and no others – ie if you can't estimate a return on your investment should you really do it?
- **Fit for purpose:** Making sure development activities eliminate unnecessary duplication and cost.
- **Focused delivery:** Being efficiently organized, using the appropriate and most cost-effective ways for those in your team to learn.

Strategic priorities

Learning activities must focus on strategic priorities and should be aligned to these priorities. How do you do this?

Is there an organization needs analysis (ONA) available? This details an organization's people learning strategies and planning processes (at all hierarchical levels), setting priorities.

Is there a departmental or team training needs analysis (TNA) available? If not, why not complete one? Its aim is to establish a list of detailed team member needs that will help you to design a training programme to meet these needs. A TNA typically assesses your team's conventional work skills and attributes, so there is also a need to develop a process for developing the unique personal training plan potential for each member of your team.

Training needs analysis (TNA)

This is simply a 'shopping list' of the skills your department/team needs to move forward and realize its learning mission and vision. A typical TNA answers the following questions:

- What are our departmental/team goals or objectives (business drivers)?
- What skills and competencies do we need to meet these goals (business priorities)?
- Are these new skills required or development of current skill sets?
- How do the training needs identified meet our (strategic) business needs in terms (of at least one) of the following three categories:
  - compulsory, ie legal or regulatory requirement, central to the customer experience;
  - business growth, ie linked to revenue growth or cost reduction;
  - employee growth, ie initiatives that support personal growth or career development.

- Are these industry-specific or general skills?
- What are the current skills/competencies capabilities of team members?
- What are individual skills/competencies requirements? What needs to change? What needs to be acquired? What needs to be let go?
- What can we afford – in time and money – to spend on training?
- What training courses are available to close skills/competencies gaps?
- How are we going to know we have successfully closed skills/competencies gaps?

The role of training needs analysis is to build a bridge between what's required to improve and the training media and training objectives, in order to facilitate the transfer of skills and competencies into your department's team's operational environment.

A typical TNA matrix will include:

- Column 1: Business priorities.
- Column 2: Training needs – options – compulsory/business growth/employee growth.
- Column 3: Delivery method.
- Column 4: Investment – budget available.
- Column 5: Value derived.
- Column 6: Priority – numbered.

The TNA becomes a commercial agreement between your company and your training suppliers. Once it is signed off it still remains a dynamic tool over time as business needs change, priorities are amended or new initiatives occur.

What is the payback?

Payback equals value. Value is derived by understanding the critical people component of each business priority. Simply ask yourself:

- Do I concretely know what my team members should be doing differently to make a big improvement to business driver performance?

- What differences in behaviour/attitude should team members be showing?
- What differences in know-how or skills?
- What (future) departmental/team changes might impact these requirements?
- What new products or services are planned?
- What potential interventions are required for compliance/ customer service?
- What potential interventions are needed to support business growth?

Learning and development resources to take action

A resource is something (a person, an asset, material or capital) that can be used to accomplish a goal. Self-development takes place when a person seeks to increase their knowledge, skills and abilities and takes action (responsibility) for their own learning and development.

For individuals this usually means answering the following questions:

Where have I been?

Where am I now?

Where do I want to get to?

How will I get there?

How will I know I have arrived?

For leaders this usually means:

- driving their own career direction and development;
- the ability to foster an environment that encourages learning and growth within the company;
- the ability to keep up to date on current research and technology in the industry and in their own professional field;

- actively participating in professional organizations to stay abreast of current developments;
- seeking opportunities to expand own skills and responsibilities;
- identifying knowledge or expertise required to meet business objectives;
- responding positively to constructive feedback;
- identifying career development opportunities – projects, secondments and further education;
- coaching team members;
- maintaining records of all development activities.

This implies self-learning, including:

- knowledge portals;
- intranet/internet;
- technology-enabled learning, CD Roms and DVDs.
- 'Experiential' learning and development:
- on-the-job training;
- 'sitting with Nelly' (learning by watching someone else do the task);
- undertaking specific tasks and projects;
- job rotation;
- secondment and attachment;
- organize a best-practice benchmarking visit;
- continuing professional development (CPD);
- action learning.

Through guidance:

- coaching;
- mentoring.

And finally, formal training:

- in-house or public training programmes.

Figure 9.1 Learning pyramid

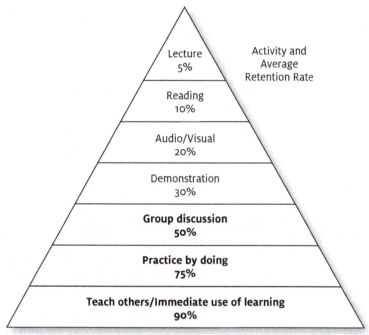

SOURCE National Training Laboratories, Bethel, Maine

The general consensus about the effectiveness of various methods of development is summarized in the 'learning pyramid' in Figure 9.1, and has appeared in various forms. This version of the diagram simply deals with how effectively students/delegates are thought to retain information. There is academic debate about the contents of this information, since there are so many variables with learning, and the initial research that the findings were based on has now been lost. However, I believe that this is probably an accurate reflection of how people absorb and retain information.

The various options that are available to both you and your reports are outlined below.

Self-learning

If you wish to simply source information knowledge portals, the intranet/Internet, and distance learning all have their place.

If you require a more in-depth exploration of a topic, however, I would suggest you adopt a blended learning approach. This could involve technology-enabled learning (another name for this is e-learning), the use of CD ROMS/DVDs, and also, importantly, getting together with others in some form of workshop on a regular basis. When I worked in higher education we undertook research to understand from potential delegates what form of training and development worked for them. Consistently the feedback was that people found it too hard to work on their own for any protracted period of time. An exchange of ideas, and learning from others was as much a part of the learning process as the material that was supplied. We therefore organized regular workshops for participants to meet for this purpose.

Experiential learning and development

A high percentage of anyone's development is through learning 'on the job'. The word 'experiential' essentially means that learning and development are achieved through personally determined experience and involvement. It is very important to get your staff to take responsibility for expressing their own learning needs. As I have mentioned previously, they also need to have goals to attain, and undertake development as and when required, not as part of a 'sheep dip process' where they are just going through generic corporate training programmes.

As a parent, one of the classic questions you ask your children when they come back from school is 'What did you learn today?' But how often do we ask our staff the same question? They are not children, but you need to get them into the mindset of learning. So during day-to-day activities challenge your reports by asking, 'How/why… did you tackle[x]assignment in a particular way, and what have you learnt from this experience?'

Training on the job

When you facilitate 'on-the-job' training, you need to be aware of how people absorb information – are they auditory, visual or kinaesthetic learners?

People use their senses in different ways to take in information and learn. Some are *auditory*-type learners – they learn best by listening to knowledge told to them; some are *visual*-type learners – they learn best by seeing pictures and symbols (or plain words); some are *tactile*-type – they learn best when they can touch an object and examine it for themselves; and some combine two or more senses according to what they are learning.

During a development session people have a limited attention span for sitting in one place absorbing information. If training or guidance is being given to an individual, the maximum time for which they will concentrate is 45 minutes, if just one methodology is being used – say delivering a verbal part of a training session, even with the use of visuals aids. People need to practise what they have learned through the use of case studies, exercises, or syndicate work.

Training on the job should always have a practical 'hands on' application once core information has been supplied.

Remember, as well, that if a person does not use the information that they have learned during a development session, they will usually forget 75 per cent of what they have learnt within three weeks to a month.

A final key point: any of us are far more motivated to learn when there is an outcome of some kind to achieve, rather than when we are just absorbing information for information's sake.

Secondments

Secondments and attachments to other departments are also a good way of developing people's skills and competencies. If a specific secondment or attachment is identified during an appraisal discussion, your staff might need to escalate a request to a more senior level, for example to you or a senior manager who is ultimately responsible for the individual, prior to any commitments being made. You or a senior manager will then normally agree the best way of discussing the attachment with the other parties that need to be involved.

Continuing professional development (CPD)

Many of the professional institutes and societies have a requirement for their members to keep a record of their professional updating and development through continuing professional development (CPD).

CPD is a method of ensuring that an individual achieves the right abilities to do their job and maintain and enhance their expertise. It includes not only improving their current job performance but also 'lifelong employability'.

As a manager you can use the appraisal of a member of staff for part of the planning for CPD. It will be their responsibility to keep the CPD record. The plan that they establish will need to be flexible and change as the job requirements and their aspirations change. It also needs to be realistic – not everyone can become the director of operations, or a chief executive!

It is important during the process that short- and long-term needs are addressed, as well as personal ones. In addition to using classic learning tools, there are other activities that count towards professional development, including being involved in a committee, reading or attending a conference. Simply getting an attendance certificate at the end of any programme is not enough. There needs to be evidence showing how any learning will be transferred and used. In other words there is a system in place to measure the effectiveness of the learning and development.

Value added will increasingly come through people, for the winners. Only highly skilled – that is trained and continuously retrained – people will be able to add value.

Peters 1987

CASE STUDY Training and development in Malaysia

In conversation with Mary Reggie De Silva, a management consultant colleague of mine from Kuala Lumpur, it was interesting to find out the positive approach that central government in Malaysia are making to encourage training and upgrading of skills for employees in the manufacturing and service sector. In her own words:

> Training employees for effectiveness is top priority for any organization to succeed irrespective of training costs. Given a choice, organizations will prefer to use internal sources so as to cut costs while eliminating the exposure of international trainers who are able transform an organization and its practices.

It is a known fact that human capital is the most important element for a business to succeed for without it any technology or system will not succeed. In an attempt to encourage organizations to retrain, upgrade or upskill their employees, all employers from the manufacturing and services sectors are mandatorily required to contribute 1 per cent of monthly wages to a centrally held Human Resource Development Fund (HRDF) which was established in 1993 and which comes under the purview of the Human Resources Ministry.

This fund is paid back to the organizations as long as they are able to justify training costs amounting to the same 1 per cent contribution to train and develop their employees by both local and international trainers.

Employers who conduct training are able to make an application for these training grants or financial assistance to defray all or a major portion of the costs of training attended by their employees. The most important factor is that the training must be in the area of direct benefit to their business operations. To be eligible for training grants under the HRDF, trainees must first be employees who are Malaysian citizens. Employers are allowed to identify their own training needs and to implement them as long as they are in line with their operational and business requirements. Under this fund, employers are allowed to conduct training either on the job, off the job or it may be a combination of both. Employers may also conduct training by engaging qualified trainers for in-house or training that requires to be carried out on site. The claims may also be used for purchases of audio-visual equipment and materials used in the training such as for the purchase of a mannequin for first aid and CPR training.

To ensure that trainers are qualified, they all have to be registered with the HRDF and must have undergone a Train-the-Trainer programme conducted by the HRDF, or these trainers must have their own certifications.

To obtain the grant, employers can select any training programme under an Approved Training Provider status and send their employees for training and be able to claim for reimbursements upon the completion of training.

As constant training is required, the objective of the scheme is to lessen the financial burden on employers, particularly smaller businesses which may at any given time be unable to train their employees due to financial restrictions at the time. The scheme also has a pool of approved trainers for organizations to choose from and it is a matter of using the funds that they had initially contributed to the scheme.

Coaching and mentoring

First of all let's look at the difference between coaching and mentoring.

Coaching is focused on improving an individual's performance against a task, providing feedback on their strengths and weaknesses, and helping them improve their performance. Mentoring, on the other hand, is focused on a longer-term, deeper relationship that is aimed at helping an individual to learn about appropriate behaviour in a particular organization, how to navigate the political climate, and the cultural dynamics of 'how things work around here'.

Principles of successful coaching

If you are to take the role of a coach there are certain fundamentals that need to be born in mind. Firstly, it is important that you believe in the success of the person you are to coach, albeit that their abilities are not currently being utilized to best effect. You need to take time to understand the situation from their perspective, and also be in tune with their belief system, values, and attitude.

You should think of your reports in terms of their (future) potential, not just their (past) performance. Coaching is about unlocking potential and getting people to think for themselves, so that they can maximize their own performance. No two human bodies or minds are the same. How can I tell you to use yours to your best ability? Only you can discover how, with *awareness*. Anyone's potential is realized by optimizing their own individuality and uniqueness, never by moulding them to another's opinion of what constitutes best practice. To 'tell' denies or negates another person's intelligence. To 'ask' honours it. Telling or asking closed questions saves people from having to think. Asking open questions causes them to think for themselves.

Throughout any coaching session remain as objective and non-judgemental as possible and ask 'what if' and 'what else' questions to prompt lateral thinking and allow the person to visualize their response options. Coaching questions compel attention for an answer, focus attention for precision and create a feedback loop. Instructing does none of these.

When I want to, I perform better that when I have to. I want it for me, I have to for you. Self-motivation is a matter of choice. Coaching offers personal control. Bear in mind the primary cause of stress in the workplace is a lack of personal control.

Coaching should:

- be one-to-one, and in private if possible;
- start from where the person actually is in performance terms, not where they ought to be;

- build on personal strengths, and aim to remedy weaknesses;
- be regular and involve constant feedback;
- be person-driven rather than task-driven;
- ensure you give time and space for the person being coached to reach their own conclusions;
- be a joint process.

The effectiveness of coaching depends on your skills as a coach, and the receptivity of the person being coached. Success is therefore more likely in conditions where:

- there is clarity about expectations;
- success criteria are clearly established;
- clear and regular feedback is given;
- there is agreement on the resources required to achieve targets;
- there is understanding of the work context;
- rapport and trust have been established.

How to conduct a coaching session

Try using the 'grow' model, which was developed and enhanced by John Whitmore. Grow is an acronym, where G = goal (what is the team/individual wanting to achieve?), R = reality (what is the current reality of the situation/issue), O = options (what options are open to them?) and W = will/way (is there a will and a way to take things forward?).

Using this approach:

- State the purpose and importance of the session – you need to be clear in your own mind about what you are trying to achieve before you begin.
- Establish and agree desired outcomes.
- Seek to establish improvements.
- Give objective feedback.
- Discuss options.

- Agree objectives and development options.

- Agree follow-up meetings.

And finally, coaching can be a win–win situation for both parties. To have the capacity to coach is not only beneficial to the recipient, but also to the coach in terms of their career progression. It is a fact that coaching competencies, based on observed behaviour and 360° feedback, are heavily weighted in the selection of managers as they progress to a more senior level within an organization.

Mentoring

Organizations can take a differing approach to offering this service. Some organizations adopt a centralized approach through HR where a person is allocated a mentor. In other organizations there is not an official system in place and people find their own mentor(s). This will not be their immediate line manager, but usually someone at a more senior level.

If you want to set up a mentoring service across your company, you need to be clear about what aims and parameters you set for the mentoring activity. Also consider how the mentoring service will be resourced, measured and managed. What outputs and effects do you want the programme to produce, and for the people being mentored? What pool of resources will you tap into for selecting mentors? They will need to be selected on the basis that they will adopt the right non-directive but supportive role. They will certainly need guidance and training prior to meeting with the mentee, so has budget been allocated for this purpose?

If you become a mentor, it is important to decide with the mentee what communication method is best for both of you – face to face, by phone or e-mail. Your style of communication should mirror the way that has been described above with coaching, but in many cases there could be a straightforward dialogue where you are simply describing the 'political agenda' within an organization, or giving them advice with any administrative, or technical problems. Your role at times will be to help with advice if the mentee has problems with a particular individual they have to work with, in other words act as a surrogate parent. With this hat on you could also explore with them their aspirations and concerns with regard to their career development.

CASE STUDY   FM Global

FM Global is a loss-prevention engineering organization whose client base is over one-third of the Fortune 1,000 size companies.

They have a particularly robust development programme for all their new hires, which involves self-study, shadowing more senior colleagues and formal classroom-based development, with part of this being delivered at their head office, FM Global Norwood, Massachusetts, USA.

The interesting part of their development programme is their approach to mentoring. Every new hire is paired with a mentor for the entire duration of their formal training, which takes about a year and a half. The mentor not only compounds their knowledge in basic field engineering skills, should it be required, but also aids with report writing and handling their relationships with internal and external clients. Optionally, each new hire could have up to ten mentors, each offering a different area of expertise during this lengthy induction period.

SOURCE *Asia Insurance Review* (2010)

Formal training

There are certain occasions with gaining professional knowledge and development when it is pertinent to attend an in-house or public training programme. This category is self-explanatory. As a manager it is always important to ask any of your reports who have attended a training session 'What did you learn?', 'How are you going to apply that information?', 'What action plan have you developed?' Keep a copy of the action plan yourself and build this into your performance management dossier for that particular person.

As you can see, there is a broad range of options that can be called on to develop both yourself and those in your company.

Creating a learning environment is essential for organizations to survive. Why is this? So often a company has been set up and been successful as a result of a few core products or services. They will gain market share, but within the ever-increasingly competitive environment new entrants can rapidly enter the market and under-cut on price or the range of added-value services they can offer. The buying behaviour of customers can also change. This means staff at all levels need to challenge the status quo, ask questions, be customer focused and keen to learn, in order for your organization to be one step ahead of the competition.

Tips and techniques

Developing others

Find out what motivates people in your team. What projects or part of an activity do they particularly thrive on doing? Do they shine in these areas? Explore their perceptions, and press them to push the boundaries in what they do, and how they do it.

Tailor learning and development to suit their style, and target their unique development needs.

Create and maintain a development folder for each person in your team. Make short notes about what has gone well, and where there is room for improvement during your observations of day-to-day interactivity. Include sources of information for them to follow up to gain knowledge – this could be press cuttings, journals or web pages, or visiting a peer group colleague in another department.

People learn from experience, exposure and from being taught. Be sure to include a learning objective with every stretch assignment you delegate. Make them aware in advance of what they should be looking to learn during the process.

Invite clients or others from different departments or teams to join one of your meetings to share their experiences.

Develop a team blog or wiki; monitor for opportunities to guide the team's thinking or behaviour.

And how about your personal development?

Tips and techniques

Developing yourself

Gain feedback from others – use a 360° feedback methodology to find out where there is room for improvement.

Work out how you prefer to learn (is it through reading, by using web-based information, experience, hands-on activity, or talking to others?).

Prioritize your own development, and set goals/timelines for learning.

Learn through working on different projects with people from different functions, seeking out methods or tools that you can apply to your own circumstances.

As a leader, show curiosity – talk to others to learn, and trust that your reports will emulate your behaviour.

Examine how a team in your company has achieved success, and how you might emulate this.

Read trade press information and look towards new sources of gaining information and knowledge via the internet. Monitor your competition using Google Alert.

Be part of a professional body or association. This will also provide a further range of ideas and activities to support professional development.

Network by attending conferences with other professionals from a similar environment.

Agree to mentor one or two school-age potential members of staff. Challenge yourself by choosing someone from, for example, a different generation, function, or ethnic background, realizing how much you can learn from them as well.

Broaden your outlook by joining an external organization, eg a charity, school governor's board.

Identify an online community, such as LinkedIn, to share the different challenges you are faced with, to see if other people's experiences and knowledge can help you take things forward.

Write down the ten most important things you have learned. Next to each thing you have learned note what you did to learn it. Do you know? Was it on a training programme, through experience of copying an approach you have seen working elsewhere? Bear all of this in mind when developing your personal development plan.

Key tasks

- If you don't have one, get yourself a personal coach. This should be someone you trust and respect. Meet them at least once a month to ask those questions you'd like to ask but never do.

- Are you a coach to members of your team? If not, become one.

- Do you have an external mentor? Get one if you don't.

- Do you and your team members have an up-to-date individual development plan and do you work to meet what's written in it? If not, start today.

- Review the variety of options that you are using for developing yourself and your team. See if it might be best to use different approaches, for example, using coaching instead of technology-based training, or getting an experienced person in your team to take over part of the development activities you are currently undertaking.

- Make sure that learning sticks, ie when doing behavioural training phase it, to ensure required behaviours are tested and meet your requirements.

10

Proactive conflict management

Introduction

Conflict means disagreement, to battle, to be at odds. It seems to be an inevitable part of human interaction and occurs (at home or at work) when an individual's needs, desires, values or intentions are in opposition with those of another person (or group). This definition suggests that those involved see their goals as incompatible and the achievement of these goals as being interfered with. Sometimes these differences are real, at other times they are imagined. Either way, the persons involved must see differences and believe they are important for conflict to emerge. If there are no differences there is no motivating force for conflict.

The potential for conflict exists everywhere. At some time or other, we all find ourselves in situations where discussions spin out of control, and, instead of cooperating, we become emotional and angry, which if not managed and resolved effectively (and quickly) imposes significant personal (and organizational) cost on those involved. When the energies involved are under control they have potential for good. Out of control they can be forces for ill.

A manager's first priority is to view conflict as not always inherently bad. If handled correctly, the dynamics surrounding conflict can change radically.

Some conflicts are relatively minor, easy to handle, or may be simply ignored. Others of greater magnitude require a strategy for successful resolution if they are not to create constant tension or lasting enmity at home or at work. If we recognize the causes that lead to conflict, we can usually steer ourselves and others away from the damage it can cause. I'm always surprised by the small things that can unleash a full-scale row, aggressive language (verbal or non-verbal) or taking actions calculated to annoy.

The stages of a team's development

As a manager, your aim is to help your team reach and sustain high performance as quickly as possible. To do this, you will need to be flexible, adapting your approach, and immediately address issues that might impact performance.

In 1965, Bruce Tuckman came up with the memorable phrase 'forming, storming, norming and performing'. He used it to describe the path to high performance that most teams follow. He said that new teams first go through a *'forming'* stage in which members are positive and polite. Some members are anxious, as they haven't yet worked out exactly what working with the team will involve. Others are simply excited about the task ahead. This stage is usually fairly short, and may only last for the single meeting at which people are introduced to one another. At this stage there may be discussions about how the team will work, which can be frustrating for some members who simply want to get on with the team task.

Reality soon sets in and the team moves into a *'storming'* phase. The danger is to get into 'storming' and not be able to get out of it. The manager's authority may be challenged as team members jockey for position as their roles are clarified. The ways of working start to be defined and, as manager, you must be aware that some members may feel overwhelmed by how much there is to do, or uncomfortable with the approach being used. Some may react by questioning how worthwhile the goal of the team is, and by resisting taking on tasks. This is the stage when many teams fail, and even those that stay together may feel that they are on an emotional roller coaster, as team norms may not be aligned with those of the organization, before or after the support of established processes or relationships.

Gradually, the team moves into a *'norming'* stage, as a hierarchy is established. Team members come to respect the manager's authority. Now that the team members know each other better, they may start to socialize, and ask each other for help. The team develops a stronger commitment to the team goal, and all start to see good progress towards it.

There is often a prolonged overlap between storming and norming behaviour: as new tasks come up, the team may lapse back into typical storming stage behaviour, but this eventually dies out.

When the team reaches the *'performing'* stage, hard work leads directly to progress towards the shared vision of their goal, supported by the structures and processes that have been set up. Individual team members may join or leave the team without affecting the performing culture. As manager, you are able to delegate much of the work and can concentrate on developing team members. Being the manager of the team at this stage feels 'easy' compared with earlier on.

Tuckman says that managers should:

1 Identify which stage of team development their team is at from the descriptions above.

2 Consider what needs to be done to move towards the performing stage and remove conflict 'storming', and what they can do to help the team do that effectively.

3 Schedule regular team reviews to determine the stage the team has reached and adjust their behaviour and approach accordingly.

Conflict in the organization

As stated above, conflict is inevitable whenever many people with different opinions, interests, perspectives and cultures work interdependently towards common (organizational) goals. For example, in any given business, there are many, often competing, ideas for how it should proceed strategically and all strive for the same goals that will lead to organizational success.

Unfortunately, the business typically has to choose just one idea, causing those involved to fight over whose idea will 'win' and whose will 'lose'. This struggle for competitive advantage can turns into destructive competition, fostering conflicts that can cause significant problems.

Conflict is only productive if it is primarily collaborative, rather than adversarial. In the above example, a collaborative approach allows those involved to offer opinions, discuss the merits of each and choose the strategy that most benefits the business – rather than individuals within it. This process focuses on what is best for the organization and uses workplace conflict as a way of making that goal happen.

(Unskilled) strategies for resolving conflict

The essential point to remember when you have conflict is that you don't have a *problem* – you have a *decision* to make.

As children we develop our own personal strategies for dealing with conflict. Even if these preferred approaches do not resolve conflicts successfully, they continue to be used because of a lack of awareness of alternatives. Conflict resolution strategies may be classified into three categories: avoiding, defusing and confronting.

Avoiding

Some people attempt to avoid conflict situations altogether or to avoid certain types of conflict. These people tend to repress emotional reactions, look the other way, or leave the situation entirely (for example, quit a job, leave school, or get divorced). Either they cannot face up to such situations effectively, or they do not have the skills to negotiate them effectively.

Although avoidance strategies do have survival value in instances where escape is possible, they usually do not provide the individual with a high level of satisfaction. They tend to leave doubts and fears about meeting the same type of situation in the future, and about their personal courage or persistence.

Defusing

This tactic is essentially a delaying action. Defusing strategies try to cool off the situation, at least temporarily, or to keep the issues so unclear that attempts at confronting it are impossible. Resolving minor points while avoiding or delaying discussion of the major problem, postponing a confrontation until a more auspicious time, and avoiding clarification of the salient issues underlying the conflict are examples of defusing.

Again, as with avoidance strategies, such tactics work when delay is possible, but they typically result in feelings of dissatisfaction and anxiety about the future.

Confronting

The third strategy involves actually confronting the conflicting issues or persons. Confronting can further be subdivided into *power* strategies and *negotiation* strategies.

Power strategies include the use of physical force (a punch on the nose, war), bribery (money, favours) and punishment (withholding love, money). Such tactics are often very effective from the point of view of the 'successful' party in the conflict: one person wins, the other person loses. Unfortunately, however, for the loser the real conflict may have only just begun. Hostility, anxiety, and actual physical damage are usual by-products of these win/lose power tactics.

With negotiation strategies, unlike power confrontations, both sides can win. The aim of negotiation is to resolve conflict with a compromise or a solution that is mutually satisfying to all parties involved in the conflict. Negotiation, then, can provide a positive and the least negative by-products of all conflict resolution strategies.

Skills for resolving conflict

Successful negotiation requires a set of skills that must be learned and practiced. I define negotiation here as a 'win–win' outcome. These skills include:

- **Diagnosis:** The ability to determine the nature of conflict.
- **Initiating:** Handling confrontations effectively.
- **Listening:** The ability to hear the other's point of view.
- **Problem solving:** To bring about a consensus decision.

Diagnosis

Diagnosing the nature of a conflict is the starting point in any attempt at resolution through negotiation. The most important issue that must be decided is whether the conflict is an ideological (value) conflict or a 'real' (tangible) conflict – or a combination of both.

Value conflicts are difficult to negotiate. If, for example, I (as a team member) believe that I should be allowed to criticize others freely wherever and whenever I want to, and you (as my manager) believe that this should be stopped in the interest of staff morale, it can be very difficult for us to come to a position that would satisfy us both.

A difference of values, however, is really significant only when our opposing views affect us in some real or tangible way. If this team member's stand on criticizing others in the workplace results in me (the manager) not getting a promotion to a role I am qualified to perform, then we have a negotiable conflict. Neither of us needs to change our values, for us to come to a mutually acceptable resolution of the 'real' problem.

The Middle East conflict provides a good example of this point. In order to settle the tangible element in the conflict – who gets how much land – ideological differences do not need to be resolved. It is land usage that is the area of the conflict amenable to a negotiated settlement. What I am saying here is that it's important to determine whether a conflict is a 'real' or a 'values' conflict. If it is a conflict in values resulting in non-tangible effects on either party, then it is often best tolerated. If, however, a tangible effect exists, that element of the conflict should be resolved.

Initiating

A second skill necessary for conflict resolution is effectiveness in initiating a 'confrontation'. It is important not to begin by attacking or demeaning the other party. A defensive reaction in one or both parties usually blocks a quick resolution of differences. The most effective way to confront the other party is for the individual to state the tangible effects the conflict has on him or her.

Listening

After the 'confrontation' has been initiated, you must be capable of hearing the other's point of view. If the initial statement made by the other person is not what you were hoping to hear, defensive rebuttals, a 'hard line' approach or justifications often follow, which can lead to argument-provoking replies. This should be avoided. Remember that justifications are answers to questions *not* asked.

You (as the person confronting the issue) should not attempt to defend yourself, explain your position, or make demands or threats. Instead, you must be able to engage in the skill termed 'reflective' or 'active' listening. You should listen, reflect and paraphrase or clarify the other person's stand. When you understand and have interpreted the other's position to their satisfaction, you can again present your own point of view, being careful to avoid value statements and to concentrate on positive outcomes.

Usually, when you 'actively' listen to the other person, that person lowers their defences and becomes, in turn, more ready to hear another (ie your) point of view. Of course, if both persons are skilled in active listening, the chances of successful negotiation are far more likely.

In the above example, the team member and manager were negotiating as if they were equals. In real life, the manager has power (see later in this chapter), which may make the team member reluctant to raise concerns. The same reluctance might exist among other team members, who may be unlikely to deal with conflict for fear of being perceived as troublemakers.

Problem solving: A consensus decision

The final skill necessary for success is the use of a problem solving process to negotiate a consensus decision. The steps in this process are simple and easy to apply:

Step 1. Clarifying the problem or nature of the conflict: What is the tangible issue or underlying factors of the conflict? Identify the stage of the conflict.

Step 2. Generating and evaluating a number of possible solutions: Often these two aspects should be done separately. First, all possible solutions should be raised in a brainstorming session. Then, each proposed solution should be evaluated.

Step 3. Agreeing together (not voting) on the best solution: Choose the appropriate actions or the one solution most acceptable to all parties to resolve the conflict.

Step 4. Planning the implementation of the solution: How will the solution be carried out? When?

Step 5. Finally, planning for an evaluation of the solution: After a specified period of time. This last step is essential. The first solution chosen is not always the best or most workable. If the first solution has flaws, the problem-solving process should be begun again at Step 1.

Since negotiation is the most effective of all conflict-resolution strategies, the skills necessary to achieve meaningful negotiation are extremely important in facing inevitable conflicts.

Stopping conflict from starting

It goes without saying that conflict can ultimately be expensive and time-consuming. A manager's role is to ensure that conflict does not reach a total breakdown in communication stage. This means going beyond simply training employees in effective conflict management skills or setting up procedures to resolve specific kinds of dispute.

A common approach is to focus on interests rather than positions. For example, if a team member claims that a manager unacceptably interfered with a project, while the manager says plans were not communicated properly, they are likely to remain at stalemate.

However, underlying these positions are interests, and in separating the two, a manager can resolve the conflict. In the example above, the team member's interest may have been to work with a level of autonomy, while the manager may have wanted a clear plan for the project. By focusing on such interests rather than defending positions, the team member may agree to provide a plan for the project (meeting the manager's main interest) and the manager will trust the team member to handle the details (meeting the team member's main interest), producing a mutually agreeable outcome.

Another way to stop conflict from starting is to be honest and admit a fault or error, and not try and bluff your way through it. This can really help since:

- It takes the wind from the other party's sails, defusing the impulse to attack.

- By and large people like to be helpful, if only to clock up favours to be repaid later.

Conflict can also be avoided by keeping a sense of proportion, and by identifying and dealing with those little irritants immediately before they grow into major problems. So impress upon yourself and those around you that when a problem arises:

- Analyse the problem, not those involved.

- Protect your stakeholders (if only to give them the earliest possible warning of non-performance, so they can take avoiding action).

- Learn from the experience (get something positive out of potentially negative situations).

Handling a conflict situation

Nothing will ever change until you, the manager, communicate your thoughts or decisions. Your role in any conflict situation with team members or others is to say *'yes'* to the person and *'no'* to the problem. Your starting point must be to find a common viewpoint between yourself and those involved. Handling a conflict actually means handling the power of your position. Your questions to resolve any conflict and to find a joint solution should focus on:

- defining conflict causes;
- understanding points of view;
- clarifying preferences;
- examining alternatives;
- gaining commitment to improvement and change.

For example:

1 Your acknowledgment and listening is a first sign of respect and sincerity for the other person(s).

2 Secure their 'yes' to the situation. This might be the first yes after a number of nos. Ask 'Do you agree that we are in conflict?' or 'Do you agree that we have a problem?' or 'Do you agree that we are now in disagreement over this point?'

3 Look to the future and secure their 'yes' to commitment to addressing the conflict. Ask 'Are you prepared to do everything possible to solve the problem with me?'

4 Get straight to the point by recognizing and estimating the forces in play. Say 'This is within your authority: you can do this or that… this is within my authority: I, on my part, could well do this or that…'

5 Now ask 'What do you propose now happens to resolve this issue? Where is our halfway point (or common ground?)'

6 Finally, jointly agree specific and timed goals and the way forward – the next steps.

Handling a problem with a team member

In essence this is a reprimand session. If you don't correct team members' or others' mistakes, that is an even bigger mistake. You must see this meeting as a means to help someone; to help them improve. In effect a reprimand session is an appraisal session.

The meeting must start with this positive attitude.

1 Stress the importance of the discussion (if appropriate).

2 Gain agreement with the principle. Does the team member understand and agree with the principle, rule or known policy? You must never be personal.

3 Communicate the facts that have been verified briefly and candidly. Do not threaten or accuse. Communicate the decision you seek.

4 Gain their commitment by asking 'Can I count on you addressing this issue so that we never have to discuss this again?'

5 Ask them 'What do you suggest is done to rectify this? How can I assist?'

6 Agree with your team member a written action plan.

7 Follow up in order to control, assist and/or praise. The more you do this and control (to compliment), the less you need to reprimand.

Let's look at this approach in action. Take the example of a team member being rude to or disagreeing with others in public:

- 'Hello John, thanks for coming to see me. I have asked to see you as I have something important to discuss with you.'

- 'Before I get to the issue I need to ask you a question. Do you agree that people should treat others as they themselves would like to be treated?' Secure their 'yes' response.

- 'I'm glad you said yes. This morning I heard you talking with X in the middle of the office when you loudly disagreed with their opinion. You came across, to me at least, as a bully not prepared to listen to their point of view. This is something I never want to see happen again. The reasons for this are...'

- 'Can I count on you not repeating this ever again in this office?'

- 'What do you suggest you do to ensure this? How can I help?'

- Agree an action plan in writing. 'Let's meet again here tomorrow at 3 pm for 30 minutes. Please think about one or two specific steps you will take to address this.'

Organizational systems and conflict

People in an organization are often unaware of organizational conflict resolution systems and procedures. In fact, many of these can actually limit the effectiveness of conflict resolution. Consider your own organization; is there an integrated conflict-handling system in place? Is it transparent, well known and used?

Some pragmatic advice: be wary of placing the dispute resolution within the senior hierarchy. This often discourages individuals from discussing conflict. For example, in many organizations the dispute resolution process is one in which a senior manager is the formal arbiter of conflicts. However, if this senior manager is also responsible for performance evaluations, promotions and discipline, some team members may be reluctant to seek arbitration for fear that it might damage their job aspirations.

Arbitration or handling conflict between others

Businesses have long recognized the value of arbitration for disputes at work and with suppliers and clients. For a manager, the goals of arbitrating a confrontation or conflict between others are:

- to solve the problem;

- to salvage the person;

- to strengthen the relationship.

If a confrontation is handled properly, it can actually strengthen a relationship. If not, it can end it. So what are essentials?

1 Grab a pad and bring all those involved together. If you don't, the whole story will never be known accurately. It is critical that you get all the facts straight.

2 Ask for details and get the facts from each person involved. Don't rely on 'hearsay' or general impressions, or you will invite emotion-laden rebuttals and counter-attacks. Get each person's side of the story. Give each a chance to explain and don't interrupt. There may be circumstances you know nothing about and you may even be part of them.

3 Identify sincerely with all involved. They must realize that you are genuinely interested about and sympathetic with each person.

4 Ask yourself (a) Have I contributed to this problem? (b) Are there any circumstances I have overlooked?

5 Relate the incident back and state the facts back as you understand them to be. Then ask the person to verify them, or fill in any missing information.

6 Be precise about the problem. Don't beat around the bush with incidentals.

7 Ask each person if they are committed to reaching a solution. If yes, then ask for a (practical) remedy from everyone involved that will lead to a win–win solution for all. Ask what they expect you to do about the problem.

8 Be sure to keep comprehensive records. The better your documentation (how, when, what, why, who was involved and the actions to reach a positive conclusion, etc) the more balanced and productive the confrontation will be.

9 Ask everyone not to harbour a grudge or to internalize their anger. Remind everyone that they were angry and frustrated about the situation, not with those involved personally.

10 Once this is dealt with ask if each person considers this 'matter is now closed'. Get them to shake hands.

Never arbitrate while you are angry. If you need to, delay it until you have cooled down! When you are angry, take a lesson from space exploration – always count down, before you blast off! Finally, if you have to arbitrate, make sure you address the performance or attitude or behaviour and not the persons involved.

Key tasks

- Ensure the emphasis is on solving problems and not blaming individuals.

- There should be tolerance for conflict, with an emphasis upon resolution. Grasp the nettle and solve problems/conflict immediately. They won't go away. Ensure conflict is openly discussed, resulting in growth or learning.

- Ensure the giving and receiving of constructive feedback is a team norm.

- Ensure team members' views of each other are not hidden and 'corridor conversations' are frequent.

- Develop team trust; ensure team members are willing to disclose and discuss their feelings, attributes and emotions.

11

Problem solving through project management

Introduction

In our fast-changing world, finding the time for solutions can be challenging. Problem solving requires a 'solutions' thinking attitude. Facts and knowledge can only go so far. Tough problem solving and quality improvement requires the ability to define the true problem, analyse the possible causes, create options, select the most feasible option, and then implement it.

Problems occur in every organization. Mistakes are made. Of course you want to minimize mistakes happening; this could be by getting people up to speed through training, transferring part of a person's workload to someone else who is more competent in a particular area, etc. As a manager it is your role to actively encourage people to come up with ideas for improvement, and identify problem areas, not just 'push things under the carpet' because 'things have been done a certain way in the past'. So how can you create an environment for continuous improvement (Kaizen) to flourish?

> **Tips and techniques**
>
> ## Creating a continuous improvement (Kaizen) environment
>
> 1　Discuss improvement ideas at team meetings each week.
>
> 2　In your department/team have a pinboard or place for all to write ideas for discussion.
>
> 3　Build suggestion making and recommendations for improvement into your appraisal process by asking 'What do you propose?' type questions.
>
> 4　Focus on the customer.
>
> 5　Acknowledge problems openly.
>
> 6　Create a 'no blame' environment.
>
> 7　Encourage a supportive attitude in your team.
>
> 8　Develop self-determination through enablement/ empowerment.
>
> 9　Keep everyone up to date with information.
>
> 10　Develop skills and competencies, creating a learning environment.
>
> 11　Manage projects cross-functionally.
>
> 12　As the manager, accept ultimate responsibility for your projects and activities.

So the first step is to create an environment that encourages people who report into you to suggest ideas for improvement, and highlight the problem areas that they believe need to be rectified.

In reality, when something goes wrong, do you look for a solution or a cause? How much time do you and your team spend 'fire fighting'? Do you find that you are reacting to events, and that you never seem to have time to get to the root cause of problems?

Norman Vincent Peale, the champion of positive thinking, said 'When a problem comes along, study it until you are completely knowledgeable. Then find that weak spot, break the problem apart, and the rest will be easy.'

So with this in mind, let's look at a proven methodology that you can use for both problem solving and quality improvement activities.

Problem solving and quality improvement process

Use a simple continuous improvement instrument – the PDCA cycle.

Plan – look forward, identify, understand.

Do – appropriate and relevant action.

Check – monitor and evaluate effects.

Act – promote feedback to upstream teams.

Figure 11.1   The Deming wheel

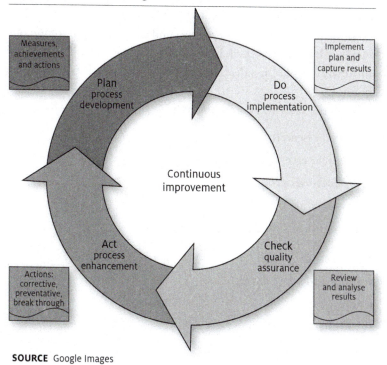

SOURCE Google Images

The concept of the PDCA cycle was originally developed by Walter Shewhart, the pioneer statistician who developed statistical process control in the Bell Laboratories in the USA during the 1930s. In the late 1950s it was taken up and promoted by the quality guru Dr W. Edward Deming, and has been subsequently known by many as the Deming Wheel (Figure 11.1). This approach was proposed as a way of analysing and measuring the sources of variations that cause products to deviate from customer requirements. It is now used for continuous-improvement and general problem-solving activities, not just for variations on a production line. PDCA can deliver 'quick fixes' typical of Western management approaches, but it also works well for incremental/continuous process improvements typical of Eastern management approaches.

Let's look at each step in the cycle.

Step 1 Plan

The planning stage takes quite a lot of clarification in comparison to the other stages, so 'hold on to your hats'!

At the planning stage you have to undertake research to find out what needs to be improved. In big-picture terms you will obtain this information from the sales and marketing area, or through process monitoring.

From the sales and marketing area:

- market research;
- opinion/perception surveys;
- product-user groups;
- customer meetings.

From process monitoring:

- process mapping;
- cause and effect diagrams;
- flow charts;
- run charts;

- Pareto diagram;

- Fishbone diagram.

So what are some typical problem-solving or quality-improvement activities that you might find happening in an organization?

- A car factory engineering department: looking to improve road holding and reduce air resistance, engine wear and fuel consumption.

- A production department: improvements in cleanliness, materials maintenance, machine efficiency, zero production defects, no breakdowns.

- A marketing department: reviewing price, assortment, attractiveness and service.

- A distribution centre: looking to ensure delivery on time, with no wrong components, and the right quantities.

Set goals

Once you have identified the problems to solve or improvements you wish to make, you must identify the vital few to work with. The 'vital few' is based on the 80/20 Pareto principle. This principle was named after an Italian, Vilfredo Pareto, who established that 80 per cent of the wealth of any nation is invariably owned by 20 per cent of the population. So transferring this to the business world, you will probably find that most of your issues will come from a small number of causes. You could also note that most of your complaints come from a small number of customers, not the majority.

You must set goals before you take action. The purpose of goals is to keep you on track, motivated, and focused on the actions you need to take. These goals need to be SMART or, as has been more recently used, SMARTER.

SMART	What this means:
Specific:	giving a clear description of what needs to be resolved
Measurable:	in terms of quality, quantity, and cost
Achievable:	including gaining the agreement of the manager and team

Relevant: specifying the business need to be satisfied

Time bound: in terms of completion date

Ethical, Exciting or Evaluated
Reviewed or Rewarded

So to see SMART in action, let's take the case of a UK leisure and parks facility to see what they wanted to review and improve, if necessary, as far as quality was concerned. In Table 11.1 below you will see how they used SMART objectives to clarify the assignment.

CASE STUDY A leading UK leisure and parks facility

Table 11.1 How can SMART objectives be used?

Element	Explanation	Example	Who	When due
Access	Ease and convenience of accessing the service	Nationwide network of offices and sub-offices, open at convenient times, emergency telephone access and 24/7 Internet access	JJ	30 March
Communication	Keeping customers informed in a language they understand; listening to them; acting on dissatisfaction; adhering to good practice in consultation and involvement processes	Plain English communications material available widely, tailored to specific groups (ethnic, sight impaired); suggestions, commendations and complaints system	NA	15 April

(continued)

Table 11.1 *(Continued)*

Element	Explanation	Example	Who	When due
Competence	Skills and knowledge to provide the service	Staff know and are able to do the job	HR	1 March
Courtesy	Politeness, respect, consideration and friendliness	Staff are friendly and polite	L&D	1 May
Credibility	Trustworthiness, reputation and image	The organization is respected in the wider community and staff generate a feeling of trust with their customers	L&D	1 May
Reliability	Providing consistent, accurate and dependable service as promised	Performance standards are met or exceeded; we maintain accurate records; we do things right first time; we keep our promises and stick to deadlines	TP	1 June

(continued)

Table 11.1   *(Continued)*

Element	Explanation	Example	Who	When due
Responsiveness	Being willing and ready	We resolve problems quickly; we mobilize to provide service when needed quickly around the customers' needs rather than our own administrative convenience	TP	1 June
Security	Physical safety, financial security, confidentiality	Services are provided in a safe and secure manner	JJ	1 June
Tangibles	The physical aspects of service, eg welcoming office environment and facilities	Our office facilities are fit for users	HR	1 March
Understand the customer	Knowing individual customer needs; relationship management	Services are tailored where practical to meet individual needs; we survey our customers regularly; customers believe they have a good quality of relationship with us	L&D	1 May

They were specific in identifying the key elements of their business working relationships, followed by an example that was relevant to their environment. A specific person was then identified who would take things forward and measure in terms of quality, quantity and cost, and they made activities time bound.

Now that you have clarified what the problem is, you need to think of a variety of approaches you might adopt to take things forward.

In terms of reaching a solution, you have to get people to think creatively, thinking outside the box, and also have the capacity to get to the root cause of the problem, to reach the 'Aha!' moment.

Reaching a solution

Running a brainstorming session

Running a brainstorming session is a quick way of flushing out ideas for improvement, or assessing needs during problem-solving activities. The idea is to have a complete free flow of information, captured on a flipchart or whiteboard by the facilitator. If this is you, keep the ideas flowing by using words of encouragement – 'Great!', 'Keep going, this is excellent!', 'Who can think of another approach?'

The process itself:

- Define and agree the objective of the session.
- Agree a time frame, and brainstorm ideas and suggestions for improvement.
- Batch ideas together, name the category, condense and refine information.
- Analyse the results.
- Prioritize options/rank list as appropriate.
- Agree actions and timescales.

No one is allowed to criticize anyone else's ideas, or make adverse comments about the ideas that have been suggested.

Freewheeling is positively welcomed – the wilder the better! People are encouraged to say *whatever* comes into their mind – the more peculiar the idea the better. Having such freedom to say anything and everything helps to stimulate more and more ideas.

The greater the number of ideas generated, the more likelihood there is of some/one of them being a winner.

Combinations/improvements should be encouraged – people should suggest how ideas of others can be improved upon, or how two ideas can be joined together to create an even better one.

Other brainstorming approaches:

Fantasy variation: The brainstormers are each asked to contribute their fantasy solution to a problem – a solution that pays no regard whatsoever to the constraints of reality. Each fantasy is then brainstormed – briefly – until a realistic idea is developed.

Stop and go: Brainstorming involves breaking the session into segments. The group is given a time limit in which to generate ideas (say, three minutes). There's then a break of, say, five minutes during which complete silence is maintained. The pause helps ideas to germinate. Repeat the process as required.

Round robin: Brainstorming sessions involve group members putting forward their ideas in turn, rather than in a spontaneous, random fashion.

Buzz sessions: These are useful if lots of people are involved. Everyone is made aware of the problem areas/issues to be discussed and then the large group is divided into smaller brainstorming groups. Each group, with its own leader/facilitator, etc, brainstorms the issue in the conventional way. At the end of the session, the group selects the best idea(s) and the leader presents them to the other groups. The best ideas from the whole group are carried forward.

One proven, successful process for brainstorming is to take two flipcharts, and put at the top of one sheet of paper Step A and on the other sheet Step B.

Starting on the Step A flipchart, imagine that you have been asked to lead an innovation group, to come up with some positive ideas to move your organization forward. Begin by brainstorming, as described above.

Move on to the Step B flipchart and agree your evaluation criteria. For example these might be:

- quality of service;
- innovation;
- organizational issues;
- cost-effectiveness.

You would then use these four criteria as a 'filter' for your ideas. If an idea scored highly against all four criteria, the chances are that it would be worth taking forward.

It is important to remember, though, that some ideas might only meet one of the criteria, but they could be so positive in that one area that they should also be taken forward.

If you want to know more about creative thinking, check out Edward de Bono's *Six Thinking Hats* (1999). This is an excellent instrument to use with a group when you find yourself getting bogged down at a certain point during problem-solving activities.

Tips and techniques

What encourages creativity?

- People are encouraged to take risks – *thoughtfully*!
- Colleagues at all levels are *supportive* of creativity.
- Colleagues at all levels respond *positively* to new ideas.
- Creativity is *rewarded*.
- *Resources*, both financial and non-financial, are available.
- Different viewpoints are *encouraged*, not just tolerated.
- *Time* is made for creativity.
- The overwhelming atmosphere is one of *fun*!

Getting to the root cause of the problem

There are occasions when the cause of the problem needs to be explored in more depth, so how do you do this? A simple device used in a continuous improvement environment is to ask 'Why' around five times.

To demonstrate this let's take the example of a customer who is promised delivery of a car on 1 August. She goes to collect the car, but is told it is not available. In this case there are two immediate causes of customer dissatisfaction: firstly, there is no car, and secondly, she was not told in advance that it wouldn't be there.

Why is there no car?

Because there was a delay in shipment leaving the factory.

Why was there a delay?

Because not enough cars of the type ordered by the customer had been produced.

Why not?

Because insufficient market research had been conducted to assess the demand in this country.

Why?

Because the company felt it could rely on its experience from elsewhere in the region.

Why was the customer not warned about the delay?

Because the factory did not warn the sales office.

Why not?

Because the production line leader was ill and his replacement did not know the system.

Why not?

Lack of training, lack of supervision, and lack of commitment.

So finally you have the root cause of the problem.

Practical planning

Plan the various stages and activities of your improvement/problem-solving project. Where possible (and certainly where necessary) involve your team in the planning. A useful tip is to work backwards from the end aim, identifying all the things that need to be put in place and done, in reverse order.

Be realistic about time frames, and always allow for slippage. If you have been given a deadline, plan to complete your problem-solving/quality-improvement project a week or so before the deadline.

Costing and budget allocation also needs to be taken into account, plus (if pertinent) any reporting of progress that is required by senior management.

Create relevant performance measures for assessing progress and the ultimate outcome of your activities. Do keep in mind that in many instances you do not necessarily have to have perfection from the word go. Sometimes you might start a continuous-improvement project, and find that you reach a stage that is 'good enough'. At least you would have started. Wanting to be perfect from the onset is fear of making mistakes in disguise. Once you have reached the 'good enough' stage, as you have taken action, momentum will take over. You will find that the next stage of moving towards a 'perfect' solution will be that much easier.

Do keep in mind that in many instances you do not necessarily have to have perfection from the word go.

We've heard it many times before, and it's still true: if something can go wrong, it will. We all must learn to figure out ahead of time where your problem-solving effort is vulnerable and develop appropriate contingency plans. Start on this as soon as you begin the problem-solving effort, making it a normal part of defining a problem.

Vulnerabilities (risks) are all the things that can prevent your problem-solving project from succeeding. Typical vulnerabilities include changing priorities, inadequate resources (people, money, time), lack of senior management sponsorship, staff turnover, key players unable or unwilling to participate, other projects not getting completed on time, economic change, etc. Of course, the list will be different for each problem, and the probability that any particular vulnerability will occur varies as well. The key is to identify them, and assess each one for probability of occurrence and impact on the project if it should occur.

Develop contingency plans immediately for any vulnerabilities that have both a high probability of occurring and a high impact. You may also want to develop contingency plans for low-probability/high-impact issues. Low-impact issues, especially if the probability is low, are probably not worth significant contingency planning.

Step 2 Do

Put into effect your plans, which could mean piloting an idea, or commencing on a small scale initially. As mentioned above, you might need to make minor changes as you go because of changes in circumstances, or new information coming to light. But remain within the original terms of reference. Be sure to use transparent, pre-agreed measurements when judging performance.

Step 3 Check

Monitor the results of your decisions and the impact on others regularly.

You should also consider the need to monitor your environment. You must know early if any risks to implementation show signs of occurring. Your monitoring programme has always to include regular communication with all stakeholders and with the leaders of any projects you are depending on. You'll want to let these people know either that everything is on track or if risks are emerging that you are aware of them and have an appropriate contingency plan, and understand what implications there might be for others.

It is important as well to focus on the specific learning, knowledge or principles that can be drawn from undertaking the project as you go along. Focus on what has worked for you, and what hasn't, and how you might apply this learning next time. Also examine priorities and how they actually compare to what you are doing, in other words helping you focus on what is important.

To conclude, what are practical questions to ask during the review stage? Always ask your questions positively. Never threaten or blame! What's done is done. As was said in a previous chapter, the responsibility of a manager is to control change, ie your responsibility is to ensure that mistakes do not recur and that problems are solved quickly and decisively. How can this be done? By constantly asking questions to find solutions and capture learning. A five-minute chat can make all the difference.

Ask yourself for the team:

1 What's going well or what did you set out to achieve?

2 What actually happened?

3 Why did that happen?

4 What should we do differently next time?

5 What action should we take?

CASE STUDY   Virginia Mason Health System

Virginia Health System's vision to be a quality leader in health care meant continually thinking in new ways.

In the past they relied on traditional methods to determine where defects occurred, using quality assurance processes, hiring the best nurses and physicians who came from the best training programmes; and formed a best-practice task force that identified patient safety and quality issues. Senior management realized, however, that these measures were not enough to overcome an unreliable system that could not always identify or track where defects occurred. Having explored a variety of options in the health care arena, they opted for a system from the manufacturing sector – the Toyota Production System (TPS). Senior management visited Hitachi and Toyota factories in Japan, and undertook extensive training in the use of TPS tools.

The objective was set to find ways of streamlining repetitive and low-touch aspects of care delivery, in order to release staff to spend more time talking with, listening to and treating patients. Each hospital then chose a handful of departments to test the so-named Virginia Mason Production System (VMPS). Waste, or anything that did not add value to the patient, was eliminated from the process. For example, in surgery, at one time ten different trays were used for ten different physicians performing laparoscopic surgery. The new streamline process standardized the trays, preparing only one. This saved money, eliminated redundant processes and reduced human error.

Also, just as production can be stopped on the factory floor at Toyota when something goes wrong, staff are able to signal a patient safety event has occurred by e-mail or phone, be it as severe as administering too high a dose of medication, or as trivial as spilling something on the floor that might cause someone to slip. Management responds immediately, or the process will be stopped if it cannot reliably be assessed or fixed.

For a medical environment this change is a cultural shift in attitude. Nurses, for example, may now report concerns over the operating rooms and have the situation reviewed and responded to. In the old hierarchical structure concerns may not have been reported to management directly.

After six years of using VMPS, Virginia Mason has experienced a big payback through improved patient satisfaction, better access to physicians, greater safety and quality, and more efficiency and productivity throughout the organization.

Some of the specific results include:

- a saving of $11 million in planned capital investments;
- reduced inventory costs by more than $1 million;
- reduced staff walking by more than 60 miles per day;
- reduced labour expenses in overtime and temporary labour by $500,000 in one year.

SOURCE: Kaplan and Peterson (2008)

Step 4 Act

In the reviewing of a process situation this is the time when corrective action is taken. You might need to take some form of preventative arrangement, or standardization, to ensure the problem does not occur again. If the problem-solving activity was done as a pilot initiative, this is the moment to take it company wide.

The 'act' stage is also the time to involve others, for example suppliers or internal customers that are affected by the changes and whose cooperation you need to implement them on a larger scale. This is also when you share your learning experiences with others who might benefit from the information.

At the heart of this process is the idea that you're going to be acting in a circle of increasing knowledge. Each time that you act you're doing so with a better understanding of what works and what doesn't.

Instead of being stopped in your tracks by trying to get everything right the first time, you act in the best way you know how at the time, witness and analyse your results, correct your approach, and try again. All the research and planning in the world will never be as effective as going ahead, acting, and witnessing what happens.

Key tasks

- Get up to date through research to identify where there is room for improvement in your company.

- Get used to asking why – five times if necessary – to get to the real cause of the problem.

- Use the PDCA cycle for your problem-solving and continuous-improvement activities.

- Don't be too hung up on getting it right first time. Just take action, and this will ultimately prompt further action.

12

Developing your company and implementing change

Introduction

So you have got your company up and running and employed key personnel to build the business with you. The reality is that the status quo cannot last indefinitely. Change will occur for a variety of reasons. Globalization and the use of information technology have created intense competition for organizations, where a customer is in a position to source their products and/or services from companies anywhere in the world, based on price, quality and delivery terms. In times of prosperity, lack of development and change in an organization can be tolerated. Now as the world economy is in recession, the UK is instigating Brexit and Donald Trump plans to change well-established trading patterns, the need for change is more critical. Rescue and realignment projects will not be about tweaking business processes. Change may be the key to a company's very survival.

In good times, change is about competition, leverages, forward thinking. The best practitioners in the world are those that know how to adapt their organization during a downturn, learn, and don't forget the bad times in their future planning.

It would be easy to think that change can come about by going on a change management course, establishing a vision, finding a mentor, designing the programme and monitoring the outcome. Dream on! In the real world leaders desert you, your staunchest allies cut and run, opposition comes from places you least expect, and your fiercest opponent can turn out to be your greatest supporter. According to a recent McKinsey report 70 per cent of so-called change management programmes have failed to deliver many of the results they expected.

If anything is certain, it is that change is certain. The world we are planning for today will not exist in this form tomorrow.

Philip Crosby, quality management guru

So what kind of changes might you have to deal with? There could be a reorganization of the company, downsizing, rightsizing, a need to adopt a more flexible working arrangement using staff on a part-time basis to avoid the need for layoffs, or outsourcing of a particular facility that is currently run in-house. Technology will certainly be constantly changing, enabling you to have virtual teams, which might or might not currently exist. And of course, regrettably, there might also be the need to make redundancies.

As a manager, whether you like it or not everyone watches what you do during a change initiative. You are in the spotlight both inside and outside the company. With this in mind let's start by looking at how you can aid and support your staff during change.

How to aid and support your staff during change

It might seem perverse, but the uncertainty created by the current global economic crisis could be the best time to make changes in your organization. You don't have to justify and prove the case for change and adaptation, whereas in good times there could be more resistance. Many organizations are taking this opportunity to get rid of underperforming staff.

Change management entails thoughtful planning and sensitive implementation, and above all the involvement of the people affected by the changes. The process must be realistic, achievable and measurable. As the owner of the company, you are in a position to compel people to perform. However, when it comes to change, you're liable to create your own worst nightmare: people quit but stay; people say 'yes' but do 'no'; people go through the motions but don't perform. You need to get buy-in from those impacted by the changes, and you can't do this on your own. As we have seen in the chapter on project management, involving your team and front-line staff at an early stage in planning and implementing changes will not only lighten your burden but also create a sense of ownership and familiarity amongst the people affected the most.

Having said this about involving staff, it is not their responsibility to manage change – that is down to you and your management team, who are there to enable and facilitate change.

One of the leading authorities on the management of change is Harvard professor John P Kotter. In his book *Leading Change* (1995) he offers a useful model as a guideline, entitled 'Eight steps to successful change'. The steps are as follows:

1 **Take urgent action:** Be focused on major opportunities, constantly keeping an eye on the marketplace and competitive activity. Ensure continuous improvement activities reduce the need for crisis management, and should it occur be rapid in response.

2 **Create a guiding team to enable change:** Ensure that those in the team have sufficient authority, energy, drive and skill sets to move things forward. Mental or emotional health is also an important attribute. Emotional health is probably a base on which so called interpersonal skills grow. Have this team's behaviour act as a role model to others.

3 **Develop a vision and strategy for change:** Focus on the end results you want to achieve with regard to service and efficiency. Excite people by connecting to their values. People involved in deciding how to implement the vision must be honest, not manipulative.

The right kind of support must be forthcoming so that individuals can succeed in making progress towards that vision.

4 **Communicate the vision to gain buy-in:** Involve people at every level in the organization, by using simple and clear communication, and making them realize the need for change. Engage in dialogue with your staff, not allowing the communication to only flow in one direction.

5 **Enable/empower action:** Get the structure of the organization right to enable this to happen. Continually look to identify and remove obstacles to change. Encourage creativity and risk taking.

6 **Go for short-term wins:** Initially tackle assignments where there can be a quick successful resolution, to keep people motivated and inspired to do more. See an improvement in performance, and reward those involved for what they have achieved. Create a manageable number of initiatives, broken down into bite-sized chunks in order to recognize results.

7 **Don't let up:** Constantly review inhibitors to performance, be it systems, processes, procedures or organizational structure and look to reduce or eliminate them. Have visible monitoring and progress reports to benchmark standards and keep staff motivated, and put in place future milestones for the way forward.

8 **Ensure changes stick:** Reinforce the new behaviours and show how they relate to organizational success. Ensure during the recruitment process that new staff are aligned to the company culture. Use change agents throughout the organization to sustain change.

The leader's first job is to define reality. The last is to say thank you.

(Max De Pree 1990)

With this in mind, let's start by looking at how you can help yourself and support your staff during change.

Before starting, there are three questions any manager should ask him- or herself. These questions concern the type of change required:

1 Is the required change 'adaptive'? In other words are you reintroducing a familiar practice?

2 Is the required change 'innovative'? In other words are you introducing a new practice to the organization?

3 Is the required change 'radical'? In other words are you introducing a practice new to your industry or sector?

The degree of complexity, cost, uncertainty and the potential for resistance to these changes rises from low to high as you go from 1 to 3.

A lot of people panic when change is introduced. They want to know 'Will I have a job?' That's the first resistance. Many say 'There's no way this can work. It's too complicated.' The manager's job is to show how the changes being introduced are related to other changes or organizational strategies.

What are the essential lessons that many experienced change managers talk about when making change?

- **Context is king:** People can learn to deal with ambiguity; they may even learn to prefer it. But they need a clear picture of the end goals. Focus on results and deliverables, not attitudes, expectations or emotions. Managers have got to be able to explain the past – how and why we got where we are today – in order for people to understand the (better) future.

- **Check in early and often:** Implementing change is a dynamic process. You always have to worry about how far and fast people can move. It's intuitive – how are people feeling? You have to listen carefully.

- **Be a catalyst, not a controller:** Let the people who are going to do the work fill in the blanks between the 'big concepts' and what's happening on the ground. As soon as you can, turn over the next phase of change to the people who have to make it. That's how you generate commitment.

Eight priorities for change managers

Use your authority. This defines you as a change manager. There's a tremendous amount you can change to become an example to others. Understanding your authority means accepting your limitations; only concentrate first on areas you where you have authority.

Remember, you may have delegated a project that is operating as a self-directed team. Be sure to set your own boundaries working with this team.

Check to see how much the 'system' is stacked against you. Never underestimate that. Pick your battles. As a change manager, you have to pick which battle you really mean to fight, and never sacrifice the war over one little skirmish. You have to learn to think of leading change like working in an emergency room. If you go to an emergency room, the triage nurse decides who gets treatment first. The child with a broken finger can wait for five hours while the medical team deals with a life-or-death case that's on the operating table. Change managers have limited resources. Keep asking yourself: what are the priorities? Decide who or what should stay in the waiting room.

Any change agent has got to be an exemplar of change. If you don't believe in yourself, nobody will. Decide your point of view about the change you are undertaking and know the specific benefits the change is designed to bring. If you lose sight of that you might become dead in the water.

Every change agent has to deal with the political issues of change. That means you have to understand that being an effective change manager is about keeping on the positive side of all stakeholders. Be proactive and keep them updated. Even no news is news. An invisible change manager will be seen as ineffective. An invisible change manager doesn't do anybody any good.

A more common problem, and ultimately more difficult, is the issue of being seduced about 'staying safe'. A change manager who's looking over the fence at the next organizational opportunity isn't going to succeed. I don't believe change managers can 'stay safe'. You have got to answer the question 'How am I going to deal with the politics that may have arisen in my company?'

If you get the above points right, if you've got a point of view, if you are bold and free, you'll be recognized as a good change agent leader.

You must understand what the job of a change manager is. It's about talking about the issues that many don't want to talk about, the ones that drive the business. It's about moving people out of their comfort zones. It's also about focusing on financial performance and creating shareholder value. This is not just about the 'soft stuff'. Change agents who don't really understand the financial issues of the company aren't worth much.

If you want to self-destruct as a change manager, practice the notion of 'Don't do as I do, do as I say.' A change manager has got to walk the walk, and talk the talk. After all, if you're doing this work the right way, you're completely exposed. The moment you compromise your integrity, you're rendered ineffective – even if you don't notice at first.

All change managers come to a point where they no longer think of what they do as a change programme. It just becomes the way you do business. Personally I can't imagine doing anything else.

The impact of information technology

In organizations, information technology (IT) helps to solve problems related to data, information and knowledge capture, processing, discovery and rendering. Today, the term *information* has ballooned to encompass functions from installing applications to designing complex networks and information databases. And that's the issue. Information activities present a special organizational problem. IT is concerned with the entire process. Consider, for example, Groupware, which refers to programs that help people work together collectively while located remotely from each other. Within such a team environment *process management information* moves precisely to where team members need it, unfiltered by a hierarchy. A horizontal self-managed company isn't only possible, it's inevitable. Data and information can go straight to those who need it to do their job. Time zones and geography are no longer of significance through the use of e-mail/computer conferencing and smartphones/iPhones.

As organizations make better use of IT, as in the Groupware example above, hierarchical levels may increasingly disappear, since information goes straight to front-line employees.

The particular requirements for those working on a flexible or part-time basis

The employment model of a workforce reporting to a location for a fixed working day is now superseded by a model based on outsourcing, hot-desking, teleworking, computer cottage approaches, and the creation of virtual teams. This has all been enabled by technology.

In turn, legislation now requires companies to consider making flexible working available to employees if they request it, and normally it can only be denied if operationally it is not feasible. This means that as long as the customer does not suffer, budgets are met and the work is done to an agreed standard in a timely manner, the company should consider most requests favourably. This has resulted in employees being able to work on a flexitime basis for the hours that suit them, or only during school term times, job sharing or working totally from home if they wish.

CASE STUDY   British Telecom

A study into BT's flexi-working programme, Options 2000, found savings of 424,000 miles a week of car travel and 190,000 miles a week of rail travel. Social benefits included spending more time with the family and less time commuting. A similar study into BT's own use of (audio and video) conferencing found annual savings of 54,000 tonnes of CO_2 and £9.7m in financial savings.

Big names that have welcomed flexi-working include Barclays, Xerox and Lloyds TSB. The RAC has seen productivity increase by 8 per cent thanks to flexi-hours, and HSBC has almost trebled the number of women coming back to their jobs after having babies. Small IT training firm Happy Computers is twice as good as its competitors at keeping staff as a result of allowing staff to work on a flexible basis. Asda was a pioneer in flexi-working for its 130,000 staff. They allow fertility leave for people who want IVF, and give Benidorm leave to older workers who want to take sunny holidays. The only time they might limit the allowance of flexitime is during busy trading – Saturdays, Christmas and Easter.

There are very obvious benefits in an organization offering flexi-working. Benefits to the company include:

- There is a reduction in the office space required.

- Productivity can be enhanced, due to the employees adjusting their hours to suit customers' requirements.

- The 'virtual office' can offer extended opening hours – far longer than the 9–5 normal office hours.

- There is less business travel time.

- There is a reduction in absenteeism, which can often be caused by a member of staff needing to care for a relative who is sick, or take time off for 'sickness', when in reality their boiler has blown up and they need to get a plumber out to fix it.

- It is a good benefit to mention during the recruitment process to attract high-calibre candidates.

- It will improve the retention rate of staff.

- During any strike period, or disruption of travel due to adverse weather conditions, companies can maintain continuity of service for customers.

The benefits to an individual include:

- It naturally empowers staff and shows that you trust them, and so is good for staff morale.

- It makes people feel they are in control of their lives, and have autonomy.

- It allows people such as 'back to workers' to gear their working life around childcare arrangements.

- It means new opportunities to work for those who previously were excluded.

- There is an improvement in work–life balance.

- To be able to work remotely or on a flexitime basis will often mean the person concerned will need to learn new skills, which are readily transferable in the marketplace. So it is good for career progression.

Large organizations are in a position to allow flexi-working, though small companies could find it more challenging to offer this arrangement. For example, it could be they simply do not have enough staff to cover the phones or the front-line activities.

Moving to flexible working

As a manager, it is clear that there can be pros and cons for members of you team working on a flexible basis. The plus factors are listed above, but there are obviously some minus factors as well, primarily based around how to monitor performance standards. A manager needs to develop a relationship of professional trust with members of their team, and address issues such as fairness and diversity. Others in the team could see the flexible arrangement as unfair and putting extra work on them, for example having to answer the phones in the workplace, or covering extra time on the shop floor owing to an unforeseen emergency.

Tips and techniques

Considerations for setting up flexible working

Stage 1

- Does flexible working exist in other parts of the organization? How well has it worked? And can I expand this working option to others in the company?
- If there is a trade union, it will need to be consulted about teleworking/homeworking, because it will have to be assured that people undertaking this type of work for the company are treated the same as other employees.

- Can part or the entire workload be undertaken off the work premises?

- Is it possible to move from an activity to a results-based culture? Can clear outputs be established, plus quality standards?

- Does there need to be constant face-to-face dialogue with others in the company?

- Is the place where the work is to be undertaken adequately equipped, and does it conform to health and safety standards?

Stage 2

Once you have accepted a request for flexible working you will need to:

- Amend the employee's contract of employment to reflect the changes. Should the new working arrangement involve changes to the number of hours worked you will need to amend the employee's pay and holiday entitlement.

- Supply any mobiles, IT/telecoms equipment that might be required for a home office.

- Either you or an elected member of staff should undertake a risk assessment of the facility they will be using to ensure electrical equipment has been tested and certified, and the seating and layout of the employee's workstation complies with health and safety standards.

- If the employee is working from home, health and safety requirements will apply just as they do to those staff working in the office.

- Undertake a full risk assessment for technology integrity and security.

Stage 3

- Take into account the impact that this is going to have on the rest of the staff.

- Clarify to those who report in to you the specific arrangements that have been agreed with the flexi-worker(s).

- If the flexi-worker is going to work fewer hours make sure you have cover in place. Bear in mind there could be resentment from others in their team if they have to take over more work.

- Establish specific ways of working within a new pattern of flexibility, bearing in mind the need for performance management to achieve agreed outcomes.

- Establish a probation period for trying out flexi-working with an employee, and continue the arrangement if the outcome has been satisfactory, and has worked for all those concerned.

Monitoring and managing remotely

Monitoring and managing remote employees when you don't have the advantage of face-to-face contact on a daily basis sets a new range of challenges:

- How should you keep in touch?
- How do you ensure that performance is monitored and targets are achieved?
- What form of communication is best in what circumstance?
- How do you keep remote workers in tune with the culture of the organization, and behaving accordingly?
- How do you handle sensitive issues or correct underperformance?
- How do you keep them in touch with the rest of the team and work colleagues?

There is no one answer to each of these questions. It comes down to a mix of approaches, which we are now going to explore.

Getting the communication channels in place

You need to set up a range of communication channels from the word go, and in line with the facilities that your organization can offer. This can range from teleconferencing, videoconferencing, SKYPE, web-based technology including knowledge portals, e-mails, smartphones/iPhones, telephone contact and face-to-face meetings. Above all else, there should be a mutually agreed methodology. As time progresses you need to monitor the effect of each method and adapt accordingly.

There could be distance between you all; however, there are times when it is best to meet face to face. For example:

- at the start of a business relationship to build trust;
- at the planning stage;
- when making a major adjustment during a project to allow for free-flow interaction of ideas;
- to resolve sensitive issues or underperformance;
- when addressing decisions that have a huge impact on employees – for example during a takeover situation, downscaling, etc.

All the other communication methodologies are pertinent for day-to-day or week-by-week contact. It is up to you to establish a pattern according to the individual concerned. Having said this, it is important to respect people's privacy if they are working from home. Business calls should be made during normal daytime trading hours, respecting their need for rest and leisure activities.

Creating a sense of belonging

People who work remotely can feel isolated and disconnected from the company they are working for. They can also be unaware of the 'way you do things' – the culture of the organization. With this in mind they need to have a full induction at the commencement of their employment, and also have the opportunity to meet with their manager/team leader and the rest of the team on as regular basis, as distance allows. Naturally they should be invited to all the celebratory events that you hold – Christmas parties, lunches for new members of the team, leaving 'dos'. If there are any groups within your organization that undertake charity or community work let them know about this. When I worked at a university there were so many different societies or panels to join. How about where you work – keep flexible working staff in the know about any occasions or non-work activities that they can participate in.

Special considerations for managing their performance

It will probably be the case that people working on a part-time or flexible basis will not be able to be as productive or effective as quickly as those employed on a full-time basis. The expression 'practice makes perfect' is true. If people are involved on a daily basis in the process, procedures and throughput of working activities that a particular team or department are undertaking they should go up a rapid learning curve. Of necessity, it will take longer for those staff working fewer hours to come up to speed.

Information technology has radically changed the way that we work. Bespoke software packages have integrated so many tasks that staff would have undertaken manually in the past. New flexible/part-time personnel need to be fully trained on how to use the computer software – how to record and access information, and what written reporting system is required for interfacing with the rest of the organization, as well as with customers and suppliers. They might also need to acquire simple project management skills for scheduling work and processes. To take in all of the capabilities of a software package can be a daunting proposition for anyone, but more so for those working less than a full-time week.

With this in mind, do your best to ensure that during the induction process the key features and capabilities of the package are highlighted to start off with. Keep it simple and relevant to their future workload. Spread the learning process so that newly appointed flexible workers can take on board bite-sized chunks of information. Remember what was flagged in Chapter 9 on creating a learning environment. People lose concentration after three-quarters of an hour to an hour if there is not a diversity of activities. Short sessions and often, and building on core information to start off with is the key to aid their learning. Software packages will usually have a manual that accompanies them. This is the good news. The bad news is that a part-time member of staff just working as weekend cover in an organization can find a thick manual of the entire capabilities of the package pretty daunting! The best way to overcome this is to create a brief 'aide memoire' document that they can refer to if they are working on their own and have no one to ask for help and guidance. Put this in a ring binder, and each time they gain new information this can be added.

In addition, their manager should set them up with a 'buddy' or 'buddies' who are doing similar work, so that they can ask for help and guidance if he or she is not around. Have an ease-of-access methodology in place where they can quickly check out all activities of importance that have happened since they were last in work. Estate agents, for example, can use Encore Live with a Movement Book facility. Have discussion boards and chat rooms so that people can interact.

Managing part-time and flexible workers does mean a degree of adaptation from managing full-time staff. If they work in the field, at home or elsewhere, they could experience isolation and a lack of 'belonging'. This can be overcome through choosing the right technology and adapting management techniques. However, the enrichment of service that you can give your customers and the flexibility that these staff can offer will more than compensate for the adaptation required.

Virtual teams

Long ago the 'bigger is better' trend was established in organizational design. Increasingly now we all work across boundaries, distance, and time when communicating with our co-workers and teammates. Work has been decentralized, and now we are forming and re-forming groups. Information technology companies like Digital and Unisys lead the field in working remotely. They sold off millions of dollars worth of property all over Europe and the USA. At the time that they did this the cost of maintaining one manager in an office building was approximately $12,000 per year. When the real estate had been sold off and the individual been given a laptop computer, an ISDN telephone line at home and a budget to turn a bedroom into an office, it cost the company less than $5,000 per year to maintain this person.

Virtual or remote working can take place when individuals and groups are networked together through technology. They may be located in the same building, across international borders, overseas or at home, in their vehicle or even on a train or plane. The recurring theme that runs through the life and work of these people is 'networked remoteless'. This almost sounds like a contradiction in terms – yet when virtual teams are formed and consciously developed they can become an invaluable asset to any organization.

The structure of these teams can be leaderless, or they can be led from the centre of a network or hub when and where necessary. People in these teams have complementary skills and are committed to a common purpose. They have interdependent performance goals, and share an approach to work for which they hold themselves mutually accountable. Groups can be formed ad hoc, then re-form and disappear. These geographically dispersed teams allow organizations to hire and retain the best people regardless of location.

An employee in a virtual team could find that there are dotted reporting lines to different managers. For example, I have just worked with a client in London whose head office is in Melbourne. Many of the managers in the UK have split reporting into multiple managers in London and Melbourne. If, when working in a virtual team, a staff member finds they don't have a direct local 'coaching manager', you have to be very proactive to ensure that they get regular updates on performance and delivery of your objectives so that there are no surprises at the finish of a project or year end.

Managing redundancy

Regrettably, in these turbulent economic times you could find whilst managing change that you need to make redundancies. Making people redundant is a sad fact of every manager's life. When the economy appears to be turning into recession many companies downsize or 're-engineer', 'restructure', 'transform' or 'renew' the business. Perhaps surprisingly, evidence suggests that companies achieve no financial gains (the results are mixed) and, in many cases, the aftermath of job cuts leads to poor performance and pressure to cut even more jobs.

For example, in the case of a company confronting falling demand for its products or services, downsizing looks like a way to survive. Stock markets may react positively to downsizing announcements in the very short run, particularly when such announcements are coupled with a credible plan for improving performance. However, there is scant evidence to suggest that on average, long-run financial performance or stock prices are improved by job cuts.

Why downsize?

Effective downsizing requires clarity of purpose, credibility and clear communication of that purpose. Companies seeking to cut jobs in response to market-driven downturns, for example, can make this clear and credible by setting out straightforward criteria for re-employment should the company see its market recover. Failure to do so leads employees to suspect, often with good reason, that the market is being used as a scapegoat for other kinds of changes and this in turn leads to a scepticism that makes it difficult to implement those changes.

On the other hand, companies may also seek to downsize as a way of changing the mix of skills and attributes of their workforce. In this view, downsizing can be a small part of a strategy of continuous improvement and renewal. Again, clear communication of this strategy and its underlying rationale is critical. Employees, with good reason, will want to know how they fit into the plan, and if they do not, what they might do about it. A third rationale is one taken by companies that begin with far-flung, unfocused strategies and wish to concentrate on core competencies and ensure all employees belong in the core.

Facing employees

Nevertheless, at some point as a manager you may be faced with making employees redundant. The degree of dignity and compassion shown during termination affects the way remaining employees expect they will be treated. What's the best approach to take?

1   Give as much advance notice as you can. This allows dismissed employees time to explore options, and gives time for those remaining as well as those being made redundant to adjust to the changes.

2   Put a freeze on recruitment unless a post is absolutely essential.

3   Procedural fairness is important. A number of studies – in particular those of academic Joel Brockner and colleagues – have shown that remaining employees' perceptions of fairness during layoffs have a number of effects on subsequent effort and performance.

4   Large-scale redundancies often involve negotiations with unions, workers' representatives, and other interested bodies. Make sure you obtain local qualified advice about this.

5   Redundancy policies vary from country to country, and year on year. Make sure you understand and apply the correct legal procedure.

6   Best practice says that companies (or managers) must make every reasonable attempt to find a comparable position for employees whose job ceases to exist. Might you be able to redeploy these personnel elsewhere in your organization before looking for new staff externally? The term 'reasonable' means that you follow the appropriate procedures in your country as dictated by law.

7   Be wary of using the policy 'last in, first out'. This person could be critical to your business, and anyway it could be deemed discriminatory if not objectively justified.

8 If the process you use is voluntary you must decide early on what restrictions should be put in place to retain key staff. You don't want your most skilled employees to leave owing to their marketability elsewhere. Remember, too, redundancy is not just demoralizing to current staff. It could affect your ability to attract top talent later on.

9 In recent years there have been some awful examples of employment redundancies in which managers and executives have obviously shirked their responsibilities – redundancy letters have been sent in the post or by e-mail without so much as a thank you, let alone a personal meeting.

10 When it is time to confirm the termination, organize a meeting on a one-to-one basis. Think through how the meeting might go and emotionally prepare yourself. Within the conversation you need to state this is a business decision. Anticipate the reaction to what you have to say and prepare to handle it.

11 Prepare materials in advance, ie notification letter, salary/benefits package, severance period, outplacement support provided. If you have an HR department schedule meetings with them.

12 Offer career counselling or coaching for those being made redundant. If your organization provides outplacement, great. If it doesn't, personally help or arrange to seek vacancies through your personal or supplier network. Find someone who might help with psychometric testing of the person concerned to assess what they might offer to the marketplace.

13 Help them to prepare their CV and allow time off for job hunting and interviews.

The meeting itself

From talking to staff who have been made redundant, several have said that the meeting they had with their manager making them redundant was on a Friday afternoon. I suppose the thinking behind this is to give the people involved the time to come to terms with the situation over the weekend. Come what may, the meeting must be at a reasonable time and appropriate venue.

Whenever you schedule the meeting there are certain things to bear in mind:

- Be courteous but come straight to the point, saying they are now formally being made redundant. Explain reasons why their role is effected, listen to their response and restate the position if necessary.

- Good record keeping is essential, so take notes throughout.

- Clarify the date of their final day in their post, and when you will collect keys, security badges, and any company-owned equipment and property.

- Explain the logistics for leaving the company and provide any written materials, or explain who will provide these and when and where to go if they have questions.

- Spend no more than 15 minutes in the meeting.

- Escort the person to their next appointment, if any.

Mentioned above is the possibility that outplacement might be offered by your company. A colleague of mine whose organization offers outplacement services talked through with me the impact she has seen at first hand of people who have been made redundant (see case study).

CASE STUDY Outplacement

Declaring posts redundant, and thereby imposing career change on the impacted post-holders, is unlikely to win you too many friends! What you do next can bring both short- and long-term benefits to the individuals concerned, their colleagues and the organization.

Outplacement – the provision of career transition and job search support – offers positive help to the individuals and assures their ex-colleagues that they, and possibly themselves at some time in the future, are being shown consideration and dealt with compassionately – all of which can contribute to lessening the negative publicity that may be generated internally and, more importantly perhaps, externally about the company's activities.

Acquiring a reputation for making difficult, albeit necessary, business decisions but offering services to mitigate the unpleasant personal outcomes can raise an organization's reputation as a good employer and retain the confidence of the 'survivors', who are vital to the continued success of the business. Opinions differ on how best to announce redundancies – but offering outplacement support to those directly affected can soften the blow and demonstrate care.

When people are affected by redundancy they can feel victimized, isolated and bereft. Being offered professional, personalized assistance to undertake a career stocktake, review options and then receive guidance about the practicalities of job hunting encourages people to look forward and not back.

Outplacement support is usually a combination of 1:1 work (face-to-face meetings usually) with some group activities, as appropriate. Normally the more senior, the less group work there is. The outplacement consultant's role is to be a combination of prisoner's friend and devil's advocate – to be supportive and encouraging but also challenging, realistic and empathetic.

People find it helpful to have skills identified, options weighed and prioritized, effective CV and application documents drafted, and interview and meeting performance practised and critiqued. It may not have been their idea to change jobs – but they might as well make as good a job of it as they can!

Not everyone, of course, takes redundancy as bad news. For some it offers an opportunity for change, and outplacement gives them a structure and professional help to find the most suitable next career move. For them outplacement is a bonus, for others it is a much-appreciated lifeline and possibly the first and only professional careers advice they have ever received.

Offering outplacement is, of course, not a universally embedded benefit or legal requirement in the UK. It does have a cost to the employer and not all are willing or able to fund such a service. They either do not recognize the positives that they can extract from providing such support or they simply run out of cash before they get round to thinking about it. And when all else fails, the Job Centre Plus will offer similar services at no cost.

In an ideal situation, however, outplacement would be offered to individuals at an early stage – six weeks to three months before their leaving date – and not left until they have already left or are about to leave. This gives people time to think through their past, decide how they want to progress and undertake the necessary research and preparation for making a success of applications.

Although a serious business, redundancy and job hunting can be a mutually supportive activity and rewarding. When a whole department, factory or business closes, and often this can affect more than one person from within a family, people look out for each other. They job-spot for their friends and colleagues, highlight others' skills to them and offer encouragement on 'bad' days. And they celebrate together when someone is successful, and gain confidence that, given time, they too will be successful.

SOURCE: Barbara Hawker, Managing Director, Hurst Associates (Europe) Limited

The process of redundancy is an unpleasant experience for all parties concerned. Seek local advice for your situation as it can vary throughout the world. In the UK there are some relevant organizations that can give you guidance:

ACAS
Tel: 0300 123 1100
www.acas.org.uk

Business Link
Tel: 0300 456 3565
www.businesslink.gov.uk

Chartered Institute of Personnel and Development (CIPD)
Tel: 020 8612 6200
www.cipd.co.uk

Key tasks

- Review your communication channels for managing remotely and adapt or change the methodology according to your findings.

- In managing change go for short-term wins, tackling assignments where you will achieve a quick result.

- Ensure during the recruitment process that new staff are aligned to the company culture.

- Constantly review your priorities, and radiate authority and clarify through your actions.

Summary

12 steps to excelling as a leader in a start-up

Much of this book has been focused on the relationship with your staff. But there are other considerations you should keep in mind. Let's look at twelve of them.

1   You need to have strategic vision in being able to understand how your company can make a unique offering in the marketplace.

2   You must have a passion to succeed and be able to energize others to help you grow the business.

3   You should create a company where a set of core values are understood and demonstrated throughout the organization.

4   You will need to have knowledge of market conditions and how to exploit them to your advantage.

5   Understanding your customer needs is also key. You should develop an understanding of your customers' needs and wants. If you solve these your customers can become your marketing champions.

6   Knowledge of your competitors, their position in the marketplace and their activities is also a must.

7 You need to be able to plan effectively and recruit as the business grows, but ensure you do this before you are overwhelmed with multi-tasking and keeping the whole ship afloat.

8 As an entrepreneur you should be able to manage P&L tightly, and be able to evaluate opportunities versus risk.

9 Results are crucial. It is essential to measure the bottom line and ensure each team member brings in the results agreed (ahead of plan) to deliver your business vision.

10 Get yourself au fait with technology and consumer trends.

11 Your role is also to build strategic partnerships and alliances as your business develops.

12 And, of course, you should never lose sight of making your company 100 per cent customer-focused. Don't let the silo mentality develop as you grow, where one team or department can become introspective and bureaucratic at the expense of all.

And 8 things to remember

To summarize everything we have been exploring with regard to people management, here are eight factors to remember.

1 Create a learning environment where your people can continue to develop and grow.

2 Learn to delegate effectively, giving your staff the authority and resources to do the task or project you have given them.

3 Stop wasted and lost time by ensuring continuous improvement is practised company-wide.

4 Encourage creative 'out of the box' thinking and ensure your team always bring solutions.

5 Make sure a blame culture or gossip does not establish itself. When things go wrong – which they will – develop the appropriate approach to get to the root of the problem and ensure it does not happen again.

6 You may have to do one thing several times to get that one win. Consistency is one of the keys.

7 Build communication channels with all stakeholders that work (understand and solve their problems). Not down through megaphones and up through filters!

8 Remember today's core competence is not core *technical* competence but rather core *cultural* competence which encourages flexibility, change, learning and adaptability to customers.

Surround yourself with great people; delegate authority; get out of the way.

Ronald Reagan

INDEX

CPSIA information can be obtained
at www.ICGtesting.com
Printed in the USA
LVOW13s2245050218

565421LV00026B/491/P